Women & Money

Women & Money

Marie Jennings

Penguin Books

Penguin Books Ltd, 27 Wrights Lane, London W8 5TZ (Publishing and Editorial)
and Harmondsworth, Middlesex, England (Distribution and Warehouse)
Viking Penguin Inc., 40 West 23rd Street, New York, New York 10010, USA
Penguin Books Australia Ltd, Ringwood, Victoria, Australia
Penguin Books Canada Ltd, 2801 John Street, Markham, Ontario, Canada L3R 1B4
Penguin Books (NZ) Ltd, 182-190 Wairau Road, Auckland 10, New Zealand

First published by Penguin Books 1988

Copyright © Marie Jennings 1988
All rights reserved

Phototypeset in 9.5/11 Times Roman by
Omnia Typesetting · St Ives · Cambridgeshire
Made and printed in Great Britain

Contents

Foreword   – The Baroness Phillips of Fulham   vii
Preface   ix
Acknowledgements   xi

Section 1   – Money and you   1
Section 2   – You, your family and money   9
Section 3   – Good money management   26
Section 4   – The need for insurance   49
Section 5   – Using credit and coping with borrowing and
          repayments   60
Section 6   – You and your tax   71
Section 7   – Concerning you as a woman   83
Section 8   – A simple guide to state benefits   96
Section 9   – Women's finances and the law   104
Section 10   – You and the money machine   112
Section 11   – You and your home   126
Section 12   – Savings and investments   146
Section 13   – Setting up in business and running a small
          business   160
Section 14   – Financial planning for retirement   171

Appendix 1 – What the new Financial Services Act means to
          you   183
Appendix 2 – Your rights and responsibilities as a
          customer   186
Appendix 3 – Who's who in financial services   187
Appendix 4 – Key organizations   190
Appendix 5 – Financial problems   196
Appendix 6 – What every woman needs to know about
          money   197
Appendix 7 – Glossary   204
Appendix 8 – Further information   213

Foreword

I welcome this book. For too long, too many men – and perhaps women as well – have believed that women's financial needs could be served adequately by men. Money and finance were publicly assumed to be a sphere of life which could be safely left to men. All that has changed now and this book is part of those changes. Women have had to struggle with the family finances in many households and increasingly we are taking complete responsibility for our own incomes. The latest changes in the Budget help to push us further in that direction.

Now at last Marie Jennings has written a book for 52 per cent of the population on all aspects of money. Her purpose is one which we will all welcome: to help you make your money go further. She shows, with admirable clarity, that by spending just a little time each month on your finances, you can almost certainly organize them better, leaving you more money to save, invest or spend. This is good news for all of us.

As Marie Jennings shows early on in this book, there are four main types of women when it comes to money. There are *the competents, the triers, the copers* and *the casuals*. Everyone should aspire to being a *competent* and beware of being a *casual*. I hope this book is going to be a great success and that, whichever type you are, it will help you to get much better value from your money.

The Baroness Phillips of Fulham JP
President, The National Association of Women's Clubs

Preface

This is a book which I have always wanted to write. Why? I suppose because I am a woman, because I believe that women see things in a different light from men and that they have different and differing priorities – and needs; also, because I have seen something of the problems, worries and heartache caused to women (and men, too) who do not understand money and its management. In addition, now that we have the new Financial Services Act in operation, it is important for everyone to look afresh at their financial situation.

There are many good books today on money management. Even a few years ago this was not the case. But, as yet, surprisingly little has been written – in books – about women and money.

I hope that you, the reader, will find this a practical book, and easy to read. It should enable you to look at an old, some would say dull and boring, subject in a new way. Within its pages you will find many tips and hints, charts and references that will enable you to make your money go further and work harder for you.

There are many different types of women, and we all have different priorities. These, too, change at different stages in our lives. I will make some assumptions which I believe are fair: that women, by and large, are practical people, can cope and do not want to be feather-bedded. We do not, however, need to be talked down to and that is still, alas, happening – although not quite so much these days and, one hopes, not for much longer!

In addressing the issues covered in this book, I draw on the results of recent comprehensive research projects in which questions have been put to thousands of women up and down the country.

We begin by looking at the many types of personal attitude and approach to money – and to the type of life you lead and want to lead. The book then goes in more depth into specialist aspects of money, the way the system works and the ways in which money and the system can work for you.

In an age of enterprise, it is important that women play their part as fully as possible in the community and in business. What they know, and their concerns about what they don't know, need to be established, and their questions need to be answered where possible and their priorities recognized. In this way they will become better equipped to release their own potential.

This is intended to be a practical book, and I trust it will be easy for you to find your way around it. What you should read, and how to refer to what you specifically need to know, are clearly signposted. To get the best out of the book start by reading through the list of contents; you should find that you can dip in and out as you need, getting the information you want quickly and easily. Each section ends with a summary so that you can check up on your own position and discover whether or not you need to read the section fully.

Finally, the book contains – as two top priority areas – a look at savings and investment options (Section 12) and also a comprehensive list of references and networking opportunities (Appendix 8). For those who haven't yet heard the term, 'networking' simply means making use of the relevant organizations and people to the best effect.

I do hope that, when you have read the book, you will feel that you are on the right financial wavelength. My aim is to help you to use your money to better effect – saving you up to 10 per cent per year. An impossible task? No, I believe that, for some at least, it is achievable; and, after all, any progress towards that target is surely worth the effort! I have tried to set out how you can make that progress. The rest is up to you.

Marie Jennings

Acknowledgements

I would like to pay tribute to many people and organizations who have helped with this book.

For inspiration and encouragement to start on this daunting task I am indebted to Baroness Phillips, Mrs Patricia Lambert, Mrs Ailsa Stanley and Mrs Dodo Harris, all respected figures in the world of women's organizations. They saw the need for women to know more about money. I would also like to thank the many people in the financial industries who helped me determine priority areas to be included.

Jeremy Leighton and John Moysey of the Money Management Council have given invaluable help with research, as have Julian Shersby of the Unit Trust Association and Sally Buxton of Cadogan Management Ltd.

For many hours of discussion and reading of the draft copy I am grateful to Peter Hayes, Sarah Watson, Jenny Smith and Mandy Williams.

I would like to express my appreciation to Michael Fuller, Michael Siddons and Anne Bradford, all of Midland Bank, who have given much practical help and encouragement.

Last – but by no means least – my thanks to Andrew Franklin, my commissioning editor at Penguin; Jenny Knight, the editor; and Brian Locke, my husband. Their help, work and willing support was always forthcoming and helped enormously at all stages of the preparation of *Women & Money*.

Section 1

Money and you

INTRODUCTION

To be able to handle money effectively, to make it go further and work harder for you, there is much that you need to know and understand about yourself. You may believe that you already know yourself and your talents and abilities, and that you are aware of your attitude to most aspects of life, including money. My questions are, do you really; and, if you do, to what extent?

It is well worth spending time on these questions. The answers you arrive at may surprise you. In this section you will find information to help you in the process of self-analysis with regard to the way you handle money. If you are wondering, 'What money?', you have already identified an important factor that influences what sort of woman you are where money is concerned: how much money you have.

Later sections will help you with the decision-making processes which lie at the heart of good money management.

The section sets out to help you answer the following key questions:

1. What sort of woman are you? Are you a spender or a saver by nature?
2. What else do you need to know about yourself?
3. What are your objectives in life?
4. What is your attitude to money in your life and to risk?

There is an overall question to ask yourself before you go on: are you prepared to spend time and effort to learn about how to be more effective in managing your money to make it go further for you? If you cannot answer 'Yes' to this, there is no point in continuing!

THE SORT OF WOMAN YOU ARE

We can all easily recognize some things about ourselves; other things may not be easily apparent, and some may be difficult to absorb or accept. The first aspect of good money management for you is to indulge in a little introspection. Be honest with yourself and do not give way to wishful thinking!

You will already know certain facts about yourself – the obvious ones. You will know your age, the type of family environment you have, your lifestyle and the basic income coming into your family. You will have (at the very least) some idea of general levels of expenditure and of whether you are living within your means. You will also have some idea of your financial commitments. In addition, you will know your commitments to your family and to any job you may have. You will be able to identify the concerns which sometimes cause you to have sleepless nights. You will know the degree to which you need to be flexible in terms of planning your life. You will probably also be aware of any domestic or work patterns which are likely to change and of the effects they may have on your life and on your personal finances.

The things you also need to know about yourself to manage your money effectively are less obvious. One is how satisfactory you find your current life and lifestyle. Another is awareness of what you need in your life – what things satisfy you, which aspects of your present lifestyle it would make you feel unhappy or even downright miserable to go without.

You must find out how much money you have, and whether you are a spender or a saver. Most of us, of course, are both. The extent of any possible susceptibility to over-spending needs to be recognized.

You should examine where you stand today, and recognize where you want to stand tomorrow. And all this needs to be looked at in relation to you, your family and others around you – at work (if you have a job), at home or in regular or even casual contact with you.

FINDING OUT MORE ABOUT YOURSELF

The basic types

The Midland Bank recently undertook a series of research pro-jects to find out how women handle money (in other words, they are living up to their slogan and being a listening bank). The research examined the capability which women felt they had. The researchers discovered that we women fitted into four basic categories, as follows:

Type A
The competents. These are women who are capable and who care about money management. They are characterized by the fact that they already have expertise in financial matters. They generally have separate bank accounts from their husbands or partners and make their own investment decisions. They are enthusiastic about learning how to handle money effectively and do it well. They are by no means mercenary; they just like to do things properly. They plan ahead for next year or for the next five years, not just for the next few months. They are not money bores; they simply want to make the most of what they have. It may surprise you that women whom you know are in this group: they don't wear their money management ability like a badge!

Type B
The triers. These women know quite a bit about money. They may well develop and become members of the first group, particularly if they inherit some money or the family budget gets a boost. They will make their own independent decisions, including some financial decisions. They try, but are not yet as competent and enthusiastic about their abilities as the competent group (Type A). However, they will know all about the household's money management and may well take responsibility for bills and budgeting. They could have some privatization or other shares and they perhaps handle their own insurance. They also tend to have separate bank accounts.

Type C
The copers. These, too, are women active in managing their money, but they lack enthusiasm for the task. They cope – they will do what they need to do. They have either been persuaded or coerced into doing the job. A large number of them find the job boring. They focus on making sure that they can cover household outgoings and don't plan much for future needs. They leave major decisions to their husbands or partners, if they have them, and

concentrate on making the most of this week's or this month's money.

Type D
The casuals. This group is small – women who don't bother at all about money are a distinct minority. They are to be found at all income levels and are characterized by their casual and sometimes flippant attitude to money. They prefer to have someone else doing the money management chore for them. At best they leave everything to their husbands or partners and expect to buy what seems right for them, as and when they like. At worst they can run up debts that cause problems – or remain blissfully unaware that their husbands or partners have real money problems.

In the final analysis, the vast majority of women do handle their own and the family money – either voluntarily or because they have to and/or have had the job wished on to them.

Your sort of woman
In order to help you benefit from the research, I have tried to give some examples of the different types, to help us all recognize which one we are. To do this I have gone to well-known characters from the popular TV and radio 'Soaps'. Here is my list:

Type A – the competents
- Avril Rolfe from *Howards Way*
- Linda Snell and Marjorie Antrobus from *The Archers*
- Maggs from *EastEnders*
- Audrey Fforbes-Hamilton from *To the Manor Born*.

Now ask yourself – do I belong in this group?

Type B – the triers
- Jan Howard from *Howards Way*
- Shula Hebdon from *The Archers*
- Sue Osman and Kathy Beale from *EastEnders*
- Anabel Collins from *Brookside*
- Emily Bishop and Deirdre Barlow from *Coronation Street*.

Perhaps you belong in group B?

Type C – the copers
- Sheila Grant from *Brookside*
- Ivy Tilsley and Betty Turpin from *Coronation Street*
- Dot Cotton from *EastEnders* (when her errant husband and son are away!)
- Pauline Fowler from *EastEnders* (she does try to watch out for her husband!).

Maybe you feel this group is the one for you?

Type D – the casuals
- Sally, Kev's young wife in *Coronation Street,* but she is trying to reform – also Vera Duckworth
- Mary Smith from *EastEnders*
- Jennifer Aldridge and Clarrie Grundy from *The Archers*.

Is it possible that you belong in this group?

Now having decided which of the role models is nearest to you, take a look at how women behave as money managers. Here Midland Bank's research throws some more light on the subject. It established that women fall basically into three behavioural categories:

1. **Women as managers of money:** These are the women concerned with achieving a financial balance in the short term. They are wary of too much credit (which is really borrowing) and tend to clear their credit card accounts before the interest is due to be paid. A large number of them clear the full amount on their cards monthly. The vast majority of these women try to avoid overdrafts and getting into debt.

2. **Women as spenders of money:** These take no responsibility for the family budget and tend to require external control – either from their husbands or partners or, failing this, from a financial institution such as their bank. They frequently admit to getting into a mess – with overdrafts, and with credit and store cards.

3. **Women as active players in the money markets:** These women tend to use money as a commodity and, unlike the others, can tolerate a lack of balance in the short term to make a gain on a longer term investment. The group seems to be small, but it is growing and it is capable of developing fast, both in numbers and in influence.

How the groups in the research interrelate

Although there was no hard statistical correlation between the groups in the research project, it would appear that the second and third in the capability groupings (the Triers and the Copers) identified with the Managers in the behavioural category while the first (the Capable/Competent) were split between Managers and Active Players. The fourth (the Casual) – not unnaturally – tended to be the Spenders.

By now you will know which of the four types you most easily identify with. But what sort of woman you are is also modified or affected by your stage in life and your age. Key events in your life influence your attitude to money and its management. The research, perhaps predictably, established that younger women tended to be more casual and flippant about money, but they became more budget conscious as they grew older, when perhaps they moved away from home and took on family and home commitments.

Traumas such as divorce, redundancy, severe illness and widow-hood also emerged as critical situations for which women needed particular understanding and support from family and friends and from financial institutions.

Underlying the results of the research programme, there is evidence that women are loyal to those who serve them well in terms of financial advice and service.

SETTING YOUR OBJECTIVES

Setting objectives for your life, and planning to achieve them, doesn't need to be a chore. You could easily find it fun – it all depends on the way you set about it. Look at this basic summary of objectives for living a happy and satisfied life. Go through it, identifying those which relate to what you want from life. Read the book and refer to the individual sections within it. Find out for yourself how far you are along the road to achieving what you want from life and acquiring the money with which to do it.

1. People
   Which group of people are most important to you?
   Close family whom you live with   Yes/No
   Other family members   Yes/No
   People you work/study with   Yes/No
   Other friends   Yes/No

2. Looking forward
   Have you thought where you'd like to be/what you'd like to be doing:
     – in five years' time? Yes/No
     – in ten years' time? Yes/No
   Are there any actions you should take to achieve this? Yes/No
3. Security
   Is security important to you? Yes/No
   A lot? Yes/No
   A little? Yes/No
4. Possessions
   These include:
     – Property – home/boat/car/cycle
     – Wealth – money/stocks and shares
     – Beautiful things – antique silver/antique furniture/antique pictures/jewellery/rare objects/rare stamps and the like
   How important are they to you?
   A lot? Yes/No
   A little? Yes/No
5. Is quality of life important to you? Yes/No
   For yourself? Yes/No
   Others? Yes/No
   Who? _____
6. By and large do you think your life gives you satisfaction?
                                               Yes/No
7. By and large do you think those near and dear to you are happy? Yes/No
8. Could/should you do anything to help them achieve a better quality of life? Yes/No

Good, you've completed that exercise, but what do you do with the answers? Might you change as a result of this exercise, or as a result of experience? Consider the implications.

YOUR ATTITUDE TOWARDS RISK

Before going into matters in greater detail, it is important for you to check now that you know your own attitude to risk, to taking risks and to living with risks if others take them on your behalf. This is a knotty area and an important one. Surprisingly little has been said about it when salesmen or women set out to try to persuade you to buy this or that type of savings or investments, or to embark upon a new course of action in life or even when you take a job. Risk is fundamental to all decisions we have to take and if you are unsure about your own attitude to risk then you could be putting a lot that is important to you at risk. It is important, too, to recognize that there are many and different sorts of risks.

In addition to risks in relation to finance there are, of course, risks affecting the choice of job, school, husband or partner, the type of home and area in which to live, the make of car to buy or rent and so on. Each and every one of these risks has implications in terms of finance.

So how do you define risk, and how do you determine your own attitude to it? And having gone through that exercise, how should you relate it to money? Do you know where you stand? If not, can you find out?

For example, assuming you have a good cushion of savings in a safe place like a bank or building society, how would you feel if some shares you'd bought halved in value? Would you hang on to them on the assumption that they would probably go up again? Or would you sell them and chalk it up to experience, finding out as best you could just why they went down? Or would you be so distraught that you wouldn't know what to do for the best?

SUMMARY

- Before you do anything with regard to money, be sure you know yourself, your attitude to life, what you want from it, your attitude to money and what you want from that.
- Your life and getting what you want from it are as much a matter of planning as getting a promotion from a job if you are working. You must work at it. Review and monitor progress regularly.
- It is important to know your attitude to risk and whether or not you like taking risks or can live with risk. Many people can't.
- Good money management can and should be fun. Only you can make it fun. Your attitude to money in your life is determined by you alone.
- Many say that what we get out of life depends on what we put in. The same is to some extent true of the money in our lives.

Section 2

You, your family and money

INTRODUCTION

Having read the first section of this book, you are likely to have been able to find out more about yourself and about your attitude to money. You should have decided something about your attitude to risk and whether you feel comfortable about taking risks. You will also have identified a number of important facts about your background and your life.

This section will help you take a look at your personal environment. It starts by looking at where you and your family stand with regard to money. It includes some basic information to help you consider your position, so that the decisions you take can result in sound financial planning for the future.

RECOGNIZING THE STARTING-POINT

The path to good financial planning starts with putting all the essential information down in one place. Use the following Moneyplanner as a guide to compiling your own records; you can extend it to cover your family as well as yourself:

Moneyplanner – personal information

- Passport no. and renewal date _____
- National insurance no. _____ .
- National Health Service no. _____
- Bank _____
  - Name of bank _____
  - Address of branch _____
  - Name of manager _____

  – Telephone no. _____
  – Current account no. _____
  – Deposit account no. _____
  – Other accounts (names and nos.) _____

- Credit and store cards – for each card
  – Name of card _____
  – No. _____
  – Relevant address for company _____
  – Credit limit _____
  – Dates valid _____

- Motoring
  – Insurance – company, policy no., agent or broker, coverage and policy type, any extras or deleted provisions, insured value, renewal date _____
  – Car key nos.: ignition, door, boot, alarm _____
  – Driving licence no. and expiry date _____
  – MOT certificate no. _____
  – Road fund licence – expiry date _____
  – MOT test date _____
  – Motoring organization membership – name, no., type of breakdown provision _____

- Home/mortgage
  – Bank or building society – name, no., type, with or without insurance, type of payment (e.g. banker's order, direct debit, cheque; and dates) _____
  – Name and address of branch _____
  – Name of branch manager _____
  – Telephone no. of branch _____

- Will
  – Date _____
  – Where kept _____
  – Names, addresses and telephone nos. of executors and solicitor _____

- Insurances (see also the checklist in Section 4)
  – House fabric: company, policy no., agent or broker, coverage and policy type, any extras or deleted provisions, insured value, renewal date _____

– House contents: company, policy no., agent or broker, coverage and policy type, any extras or deleted provisions, insured value, renewal date _____

– Health: company, policy no., agent or broker, coverage and policy type, any extras or deleted provisions, insured value, renewal date _____

– Permanent health: company, policy no., agent or broker, coverage and policy type, any extras or deleted provisions, insured value, renewal date _____

– Life/endowment: company, policy no., agent or broker, coverage and policy type, any extras or deleted provisions, insured value, renewal date _____

– Other: company, policy no., agent or broker, coverage and policy type, any extras or deleted provisions, insured value, renewal date _____

– Pension provisions/insurances/assurances: company, policy no., agent or broker, coverage and policy type, any extras or deleted provisions, insured value, renewal date _____

COMMITMENTS – TO YOURSELF AND OTHERS

We are, all of us, to some extent dependent on others. No matter how much we may like to think that we are self-sufficient, that we don't need others, the simple fact is that we aren't and we do. It is most important to know where you stand in relation to those around you.

When looking at how you can manage your money effectively and make it go further and work harder for you, you should first take stock of the commitments you may have, through your husband or partner, your children (if you have any) and other members of your family who may at any time be dependent on you for financial or other help.

You should also take a look at what you may realistically expect others to do for you, whether in terms of giving you money, leaving you beautiful things in wills or helping you by rendering services. To have a complete picture of where you stand, you must look at both sides of the coin – what you expect from others and what they expect from you. It isn't materialistic to undertake such an exercise; it is sound common sense. To help you to do this look at the following list. Fill in the details as they relate to you. It will help you to complete your own picture.

Commitments – yours to other people

Under this heading, fill in the commitments you have, whether in terms of money or caring, etc. Don't forget to fill in the period of time involved.

This format may not fit your position exactly but it should help – put in your own entries where relevant.

Commitments	To (identify members of family or others)	Period/term
Share of mortgage/rent at £ . . . per month	Husband/building society/flat-sharers	Until . . .
Share of housekeeping		
Children's costs: child care, nursery, pocket money	Child-minder	Until earning or school age
Birthday and Christmas presents	Family	Recurring
Holidays	For how many	
School fees at £ . . . per term	Children/school	Until . . .

Now consider the picture you have revealed.

Commitments – others to you

It is wise also to look at commitments others may have to you – here is an example for you to adapt for your own purposes.

Commitments	From (identify relationship to you)	Period/term
Contribution to housekeeping	Mother or father	Ongoing
Contribution to housekeeping	Daughter or son	Sporadic – over next two years, perhaps

Having determined your commitments to others, and theirs to you, let us now look at you as a money manager.

ARE YOU AN EFFECTIVE MONEY MANAGER?

Being an effective and creative money manager means looking at all aspects of the subject of money management in the round, and also recognizing value for money where you see it. This relates to the value of time spent as well as the money spent purchasing goods and services.

Let me explain.

Whether an article is cheap or expensive may, for many, be largely irrelevant. The key point is whether or not it represents value for money – value to you for the money you have spent. Exactly the same is true in relation to savings and investments which you buy for money; are you getting good value? The same applies to services too.

Here is an example:

The hairdryer you bought last week may be the cheapest or the most expensive you could find. Whether it was the best value for money is not a matter of the cost of the product alone. The other factors involved include:

1. Whether it is covered by guarantee, and how easy it will be to send it back if it goes wrong.

2. Whether the guarantee includes replacement of parts alone or includes both parts and service.

3. The electrical rating of the machine.

4. Whether the machine takes a short or long time to complete its work cycle, thereby involving low or high costs for electricity.

5. Whether it dries your hair effectively and is well balanced and easy and safe to hold and use.

6. Whether it breaks down frequently – thereby causing you trouble getting it repaired, even if it is still under guarantee.

7. Whether it is robust (so that it doesn't break when dropped or overheat when used for long periods), looks good and is easy to store and put away.

Working on similar lines, try to find out whether you are spending your money on goods and services that are good value for money.

Ask yourself these questions:

Yes/No

- Do I plan ahead – for my life, for my money?
- Do I only rarely have unpleasant surprises – unexpected bills arriving at my home, birthday and Christmas expenses amounting to a lot more than I think they will, or major bills like electricity, gas, telephone, etc., being so high that I have to dip into the housekeeping money?
- Do I remember when I need to pay the insurance, car tax, rates, heating and lighting?
- Can I put my hands easily on my bank statements, insurance policies, mortgage accounts, rates/community charge, tax demands and other essential paperwork?
- Do I keep financial records neatly in place and in date order for checking payments and ensuring that all is well?
- Do I check them off each month according to what I know I spent?
- Do I swap chores such as taking the kids to school, shopping and the like with others?
- Do I plan shared travel costs to work (if I go to work or to the station by car)?
- Is every job in the home done by me and the family (within our range of skills) to save the costs of outside contractors?
- Do I regularly do (or have done) the essential maintenance of house and/or car, avoiding big bills for large or emergency jobs that 'a stitch in time' can prevent?
- Do I think of offering to do for others the things which I can do quickly and well (such as the decorating, perhaps) and asking them to do for me what I find difficult and slow (such as the gardening, possibly)?
- Do I only rarely find that I have left unstarted or uncompleted things I should have done?
- Am I hardly ever late sending in the money for bills, the TV licence and the road tax?
- Do I know my bank manager?

Yes/No

- As well as giving to charity jumble sales, do I also swap things I don't need, such as unwanted items of jewellery, for something I will use – either through swap shops or friends?
- Am I aware of where my time goes and do I recognize that it has a value in real money terms?

Now look at the answers you have given to these questions and count up your score:

- Noes: Over 7, you need to take some positive action – you're off course!

  Between 6 and 3, you are on a steady course but could improve if you took action.

  Less than 2, congratulate yourself because you are an effective and creative money manager – but remember not to become complacent!

MONITORING PROGRESS

Your basic aim must be slowly and surely to improve your money management and to make your money go further and work harder for you. How do you monitor the progress you are making?

First, give yourself a time frame. Let us say you read this book today and decide you want to help yourself. Here's how:

- Take a time frame of, say, six months.
- Work out where you are by reading and filling in the charts and forms in this book.
- Keep up to date – decide you will read at least one of the family finance sections in the Sunday papers each week.
- Go and talk to your bank about your general position and ask them for their comments (and their advice; it can often be useful even if in the end you find you don't take it!).
- Prepare and keep going your own set of Moneyplanner files based on those in this book.
- Decide where you want to be in five years' time, and decide, too, how much time you are prepared to devote to your money management. It needs to be at least an hour a month, preferably more.
- Make a list of action points – date the list and update it monthly.
- Make a note to report to yourself on your general position and

the progress you have made in three months, and again in six
months.
● Do it!

Then, after the first six months:

● Make a positive review of how well the system has worked for
  you. Revise it and set a plan for the future – the next six
  months and the next year. At the first revision you may not
  seem to have achieved very much, but keep at it. The more you
  follow a discipline like this, the more you will learn about the
  system you are building up. The more you learn and work at it,
  the better you will become. The end result should be that you
  find you are getting more value for your money.

SETTING PRIORITIES

Next, look at your priorities. You will need to set them for the
future, deciding how you would like to see your life develop. If
you fill in the checklist given below, that will start you off. Give
yourself stars as applicable. Study the answers you gave to questions in the previous section.

Your priorities in life

Stars

Happiness – An elusive quality, but it is important to
recognize where you stand today. Mark yourself with
1, 2 or 3 stars (3, happy; 0, dismal).

Quality of life – This relates to whether or not you have
long periods when you are bored or doing things which
you dislike or find repetitive, unsatisfying or unsatisfactory. Again, give yourself 1, 2 or 3 stars (3, interesting
life; 0, dull).

Motivation – Do you take a laid-back attitude or are
you raring to go – in relation to the following:
– Your home life?
– Your job?
– Your hobbies and recreations?

Star yourself for each one (1, motivated; 0, passive).

Family/friends/commitments – Are you relaxed and feeling that your relationships are satisfactory and in balance? Star yourself separately (1, good relationships; 0, poor) for:
– Family
– Friends/work associates
– Commitments – in terms of time and money, for example in relation to elderly relatives.

What do you find when you have added up the stars? Eight or more mean you are on the rails; if you have four or fewer you need to get back on to them.

The star rating you have awarded yourself will help you to see where you need to consider taking action to improve matters, and where priorities (low star rating) mean you should consider putting more into life to enable you to get more out of it.

Your priorities in relation to your money
This is another area of some importance. Find out where you stand by using this checklist. Fill it in as applicable:

Stars

Making ends meet – By and large, do you get by satisfactorily and make ends meet? Give yourself stars to find out (3, satisfactory; 0, often in debt).
Planning for today – Are you confident you know where you stand in relation to your financial affairs in the current year? This includes:
– Money coming in and going out
– Holidays
– Birthday and Christmas arrangements
– 'Rainy day' money – what sort it is, and where
– Savings, pensions and insurances – costs and benefits
– Tax – income, car, community charge or rates
– Possible problems, illness, job loss (situations in which you may suddenly need emergency money).
You need to try to ensure that, at the very least, you will start next year no worse off than this! Star yourself to find out (3, planning works well; 0, problems common).
Planning for tomorrow – Have you thought about

Stars

next year? How may things change? How may your personal finances be affected? Star yourself to find out (3 stars for a future well provided for; 1 for 'wait and see'; 0 for 'not thought about').

Planning for the future – Looking five years and more ahead, do you know where you will stand and where you will want to stand (3 stars for 'Yes' in general terms; 0 for 'No')?

Making adequate provisions against contingencies – These include losing your job, coping with major expenses in the home, unexpected serious and sudden illness and unexpected calls on you for money to help a relative or friend. Have you provided for savings, pensions and/or tax? Star yourself to find out (3 for full provisions; 0 for no provision).

Again, add up your stars to see where you stand and what action you may need to take. With ten or more stars you have yourself in hand; with five or fewer you could surprise yourself and see how much better life is when you decide priorities for yourself instead of letting circumstances set them for you.

MAKING MORE OF YOUR MONEY

The overall objective is to make your money go further by, at least, 10 per cent or as much as you can achieve in practice. How should you approach this task? It isn't as complex as it sounds if you take it gently and logically.

Over recent years, for example, it has been demonstrated pretty conclusively that we can all save at least 10 per cent of the energy bills in the home – the money we spend on gas, electricity and other fuels. So, now let us take a look at whether we can save up to 10 per cent of income by handling money more effectively.

As examples I shall take three women – let us call them Mary, Fiona and Elsie – looking at their income, what they spend it on and how they could make it go further by 10 per cent. In these examples I have rounded off the figures to make the arithmetic easy – but the same principles apply in practice, however awkward the numbers.

Mary

Mary is single, in her early 20s. She shares a flat and is a
secretary. She has an annual income, after tax, of £6,000. Her
objective, therefore, is to save at least £50 a month. She is
currently overspending £20 per month and is saved only by
Christmas and birthday presents from her parents. She runs out of
money on occasion, which leads to unplanned skimping when she
does not have enough for essentials.

Income (monthly)

	£
Monthly salary after paycheque deductions	498
Interest from bank deposit account with £1,200 balance	2
	£500

Expenditure (monthly)

	Present	Possible
	£	£
Share of rent	100	100
Share of gas/electricity/phone	50	50
Fares to work	40	35 (−5)
Food at home	60	70 (+10)
(to include packed lunches and cheaper foods)		
Pub lunches at work	30	− (−30)
(no pub lunches)		
Car running costs	60	58 (−2)
(cheaper insurance, same cover)		
Bank charges	4	− (−4)
(keep above minimum)		
Credit card costs (interest)	5	1 (−4)
(pay on time)		
Fare to parents for one weekend	31	20 (−11)
(use cheap travel, e.g. saver or coach ticket)		
Entertainment/papers	50	40 (−10)
(cut-price theatre tickets on day, drinks at home cheaper than pub)		
Holidays	20	20
Clothes	50	50
Miscellaneous (including presents, cosmetics, dry-cleaning, etc)	20	20
Total	£520	£464 (−56)

Mary could also get a further £2 by putting her money in a higher interest rate bank account. She must, however, make sure that there is enough in her current account not to overdraw and also not to incur bank charges.

Mary's new budget not only eliminates her £20 per month shortfall, but will also allow her to make regular savings and to insure her personal possessions. She will be able to start saving to replace her old car and in a year or so she will be in a position to think about a regular unit trust savings scheme.

The major changes in behaviour she is asked to make are to take a packed lunch to work, to walk one stop or buy a season ticket and to time her monthly trip home to visit her parents so that she can take advantage of cheaper rates on the train (or she could go by coach). I could have suggested that she sell the car, but a car is convenient and can be safer on occasions. I haven't suggested that she should do without a good holiday or get her clothes at Oxfam or local jumble sales.

Fiona

Fiona is a married woman in her 30s. She has two school-age children and her husband pays higher rate income tax. Fiona has £5,000 invested in a building society share account, from a legacy she received about five years ago. She is responsible for all the household bills except the mortgage, which is paid from her husband's separate current account. She also buys her own and the children's clothes. She has taken a part-time teaching job to raise the money to cope with all this.

Fiona runs a current bank account (on which she is sometimes overdrawn, for example when the rates bill comes in). She has her own bank credit card, also a hire-purchase agreement for a replacement washing-machine from a local retailer. She has two store credit cards and occasionally uses the credit facilities. Her husband has a company car, but pays for the tax, insurance and motoring association subscription for the car she uses for shopping and taking the children to and from school.

Fiona receives interest based on her building society account, the rate being that applying at 27 April 1988. Her hire-purchase payments to the High Street electrical shop for her washing-machine are based on the rates at the same date. Fiona's objective is to save £100 a month.

Income (monthly)

	£
Housekeeping allowance/earnings/Child Benefit	985
Interest on building society share account	15
Net monthly income	£1,000

Expenditure (monthly)

	Present	**Possible**
	£	£
Rates	75	75
Water rates	15	15
Electricity	20	18 (−2)
Gas	55	50 (−5)
(shorter time on, lower thermostat setting)		
Telephone	20	18 (−2)
(more off-peak calls)		
Petrol	40	30 (−10)
(share car for school, shop with neighbours; less accelerator and careful braking)		
Supermarket shopping	230	210 (−20)
(own-label goods, being cost-conscious about what is bought)		
Greengrocer	40	40
Clothes for self and children	240	215 (−25)
(watch for sales; make simple children's items)		
Outgoings/entertainment/ school trips	40	35 (−5)
School dinners	23	18 (−5)
(packed lunches in warm weather)		
HP on washing-machine (£320 cash; 24 payments @ £19.26 per month (APR 37·5%))	19	15 (−4)
(substitute a bank personal loan, paying £20 now with 24 payments @ £15.27 per month; better still, for next major purchase wait for interest-free credit)		
Bank charges	4	− (−4)
(stay above minimum balance)		
Credit/store card interest	7	− (−7)
(pay off in full)		
Newspapers	20	18 (−2)
(review papers bought, share magazines)		

	Present	**Possible**
	£	£
Drink for home	15	14 (−1)
	(cheaper wine!)	
Hobby, water colours	5	− (−5)
	(sell paintings!)	
Presents for family, etc.	20	20
Incidentals and miscellaneous	49	46 (−3)
Regular unit trust savings	20	20
Contingency/household items to be replaced/garden	43	43
Totals	£1,000	£900 (−100)

The way for Fiona to stay above the minimum balance on her bank current account and to pay off the credit and store cards in full is to move to monthly payment of the gas and rates bills. This evens out the cost of the gas central heating in the winter and avoids the very big bills for rates having to be paid in two large amounts.

Even if her budget makes it hard to avoid bank charges and credit card interest altogether, she can minimize the amount she has to pay in three ways. First, she can use her card for as many purchases as possible, thus keeping down the number of cheques she has to write. Secondly, if her bank charges less for cash-machine withdrawals than for cheques she can use the machine more and her cheque-book less. Thirdly, some banks have a form of revolving credit account – offering a lower interest rate than the bank charge cards. Fiona should find out all the possibilities and choose the best deal for herself.

Fiona can also gain by moving to a higher interest building society account, receiving £275 per annum at 5·5 per cent rather than £175 at 3·5 per cent – giving her an additional £8 per month. However, as her husband is a higher rate taxpayer, she should consider putting part of her savings into income tax free savings, e.g. National Savings Certificates (on which interest is not paid; they are revalued on redemption), or even putting £1,000 into a post office savings account (which will pay her the first £70 of interest tax-free and at a higher rate if more than £500 is held in the account).

Elsie

Elsie is a married woman, aged 55. She has a net income of
£1,500 a month and is separately taxed on her earned income.
(This will not be relevant after 1990.) Elsie and her husband run a
small company and they both pay higher rate tax. All car expenses are paid by the company. Her husband's income is higher
than hers. They have three adult children. The eldest, a son, is
about to be married. The twins, aged 22, recently left university
and now have well-paid jobs, so they are off their parents' hands.

Until a month or two ago, Elsie and her husband had very high
outgoings. All three children were sent to private schools and
were supported through university.

The large mortgage on their home in the stockbroker belt was
paid off a couple of months ago and now, for the first time since
they were married, they both have considerably more income
than expenditure. Both are careful with budgeting and so a
reduction in spending is not relevant in their case.

However, although Elsie's husband made pension provision
from the time their eldest child was born, she did not. Higher
priority was always given to the immediate needs of the family.
Elsie has, however, paid the full national insurance contributions,
so she will qualify for a state pension when she is 60.

Therefore, what Elsie must do to make her money go 10 per
cent further is based on her need to use financial products
effectively to provide some independent extra income when she
retires in five years' time. She will be able to use her excess of
income over expenditure for this purpose, and could also re-
arrange some of her existing savings. This is what she should do:

Income (monthly)

	£
Earnings (net of paycheque deductions)	1,500

Expenditure (monthly)

	£
Outgoings (clothes, share of holidays, help in house, food, petrol, outings, etc.)	900
Surplus of income over expenditure	£600

Elsie has a number of different savings; these are as follows:

	£
National Savings Certificates	10,000
Building society higher rate instant access account	4,000
Bank high interest cheque account	3,500

Recommended investment programme

Elsie needs to consider both her existing savings and her new-found surplus income, and to seek the best combination of investments to suit both. First, she needs to deal with the surplus income.

Elsie is 55 so she will be able to put up to 20 per cent of her gross income (which is over £27,000 per annum, leaving her with £18,000 net of paycheque deductions) into a personal pension plan. She decides to use £5,000 a year for this; in doing so she will save tax at the top rate of 40 per cent – £2,000 a year or £166 a month. The remainder of her £7,200 per annum (£600 per month) surplus will therefore be £2,200, which will also need to be invested along with the £2,000 tax saved – making £4,200 per annum to place.

Elsie will shop around, considering her bank, insurance companies and building societies as well as seeing an independent financial adviser who is a member of FIMBRA (the relevant self-regulatory organization) – see Appendix 4. This will enable her to make an informed choice from the plans on offer.

While the pension provision will make the target saving she seeks, there is scope for more planning in her new-found comfortable position.

Elsie should also consider taking out a personal equity plan (PEP) of £3,000 for each of the years before she retires. This will result in her having up to £3,000 per annum invested in shares. The income as well as any capital gains made within the plan will be free of tax. This will also improve her tax position now.

The National Savings Certificates are also free of income tax – which is the reason why she built up a nest-egg in a number of issues. It is therefore sensible for her to hold on to these.

The pension and the PEP will take up only £500 of Elsie's net monthly income, allowing for tax relief on the pension, so she has available a further £100 a month. She should consider whether her bank and building society savings are enough for contingencies; if so she could take on one or more unit trust savings plans. Like all equities their value and the income that arises from them can go down as well as up; but over the longer term they have proved a better way of investing money than a bank or building society account.

Finally, in the present situation of radical change Elsie should seek expert advice on the best way to use the assets and income she has available. Her accountant could help, but there are other sources of advice which come free and without obligation. Most of the banks offer a form of financial check-up; an independent adviser who is a member of FIMBRA could also provide advice.

For example, Elsie and her husband have both made wills, but there is almost certainly going to be inheritance tax to pay when the survivor of the two of them dies. This can be reduced by using their annual exemptions (£3,000 each at April 1988) for some gifts. When the children get married it is possible to make a large wedding gift (no more than £5,000 from each parent) as well. Elsie and her husband should remember, though, that they should not make gifts to such an extent that they find themselves short of money as they get older.

All in all, Elsie now needs to concentrate on managing the considerable assets she and her husband have built up over the years. They clearly have managed their business well so far; now she (and he) should look towards their personal futures as retirement approaches and with it the onset of old age.

SUMMARY

- It is important to get and keep a grip on the subject of money management.
- Making your money go further can be fun – and profitable at the same time. It can really liberate you to get on with living and enjoying your life.
- It is important to spend a little time regularly on managing your money . . . not much, let's say 20–30 hours a year. It could be the best investment of your time you will ever make!
- The problems and opportunities differ in their make-up as you grow older, but whatever your age it is important to think, shop around and plan. Then you can live your life fully instead of finding that life imposes demands on you.

Section 3

Good money management

INTRODUCTION

Good money management is all about being practical and investing enough time in not just taking the trouble to do it, but doing it well and getting help to this end if necessary.

In the previous sections you have established the sort of woman you are, and have examined your position. You should now be clear about the type of lifestyle you have and about some of your hopes and concerns for the future.

This section should help you to start to sort out the practical details. These are often thought of as the boring areas, but they can be fascinating. This stage is essential if you want to have a life that is less complicated and freer of day-to-day money troubles, as well as an income which stretches to cover more – with expenditure more tightly controlled and therefore, ideally, lower.

It's up to you to look on the bright side – at what you hope to achieve – and get on with it.

The section covers the following interrelated areas:

1. What your money is for – requirements for your individual circumstances, outline of savings and investment opportunities and the factors affecting investment decisions.
2. What money you have – in terms of income, assets and savings and investments – and what things you need to allow for.
3. You and your work.
4. The importance of budgeting – making ends meet and spending efficiently.
5. The key relationships for income, outgoings and savings and other assets and resources.

WHAT IS MONEY?

Money is cash but it is also a measure of value, the legal tender which you exchange for goods and services when you buy them. It is also the means by which the market values of different items can be compared and contrasted. Its serious disadvantage is that it is not constant. Whether for goods or services, money prices will differ from person to person and from time to time, according to market circumstances. You therefore need to take care in interpreting money values recorded at different times.

REQUIREMENTS FOR YOUR INDIVIDUAL CIRCUMSTANCES

We all pass through different stages, of childhood, youth, family life and retirement. We have various commitments to others. Our varying situations create differing requirements – for income, for security and for capital, either immediately or at some time in the future. You need to plan your savings and investment opportunities to satisfy your own requirements as conveniently and successfully as you can.

OUTLINE OF SAVINGS AND INVESTMENT OPPORTUNITIES

You can invest cash in many forms. You can place it in safe-keeping with banks, or you can use it to buy property, goods such as antiques, commodities or precious metals or to obtain interest in trading activities via stocks and shares or unit or investment trusts.

Generally the only investments guaranteed to repay you a specified amount (and to pay you a specific interest rate over an agreed period of time) are national savings and government stocks (gilts). You will find these explained in detail in Section 12. All other types of savings and investments will repay you whatever sum is the result of market pricing at the time; the factors will include inflation, interest payments and judgements of future prospects. Broadly, over long periods of time, investments in shares and in unit and investment trusts tend to outpace inflation. These matters are also discussed more fully in Section 12.

On an annual basis, income from investments can be a fixed amount or it can be variable. Some investments actually provide no income. Eventually you can usually sell your investments for cash, which is known as liquidating them. If this can be done easily, they are said to have a high degree of liquidity. This is the case with most shares traded on the Stock Exchange, and also with unit trusts and government stocks. Those investments which are less readily realizable might not be suitable for someone likely to need cash quickly; shares in private companies are often of this type as trading in the shares is done less frequently and there is no daily market price.

For the selection and maintenance of the investments most suitable for your specific requirements, you will need individual advice.

Factors affecting investment decisions

The decisions about the balance of your investment portfolio and the choice of specific investments need to be based on a consideration, amongst other items, of:

1. Your individual needs and aspirations.
2. How well your needs and aspirations are currently satisfied.
3. The level of safety you require – of capital and income.
4. The risks you are willing to take.
5. The assessment of prospects and the alternatives.

You can take decisions by hunch or intuition, but they can be helped by reliable information. There are some key factors to consider in making these decisions, so you need to ensure you are armed with the relevant information.

Sources of information

You can obtain information of a financial nature from many sources, such as authorized investment advisers, accountants, banks, building societies, stockbrokers and the media. With regard to investment in specific companies, remember that much relevant information is available from the companies themselves, in the forms of annual published accounts, chairmen's reports and other announcements. It is important to know how to interpret this information correctly. Some useful sources of information are given in Appendix 8.

THE MONEY YOU HAVE

The raw material with which to work to achieve good, effective money management is your income.

To this basic resource should be added any extras in terms of

assets, etc. You need now to do your own wealth check, to find
out where you stand.

Your aim should be to live within your income, setting some of
it aside to help you build up a reserve and to go towards
occasional items of expenditure. These include major costs you
may have to face, like paying for a wedding or a new roof on the
house and also emergencies. You need to ensure that you have
some 'rainy day' money, and to make provision for long-term
savings and investment, pensions and so on.

Now is the time to look in detail at what your income is, what
you are worth and how you spend money – how to budget and
how to make your money do more and go further for you.

INCOME

First, are you in full-time or part-time employment; self-employed
as a sole trader, a partner or a director; or retired? Do you have
income from any spare-time occupation?

Now, find out where you stand in relation to the following:

1. What you earned last year. Are you likely to earn more or less
    this year, and what about next year? Make estimates.
2. Are you and your husband (if you have one) taxed separately?
3. Do you have any investment income?

Total the income you had last year, and do the same for what
you expect to receive this year and next year. The totals will give
you a good idea of the level of your annual income. (Remember
that you may have to complete a tax return for last year anyway;
you can use the figures you need here for that as well, saving time
and effort.)

ASSETS AND LIABILITIES

To help you determine your assets and liabilities, we have provided a wealth check Moneyplanner for you to use as a guide
when you draw up your own list. As you may not be entirely clear
about what assets and liabilities are, here is an outline.

Assets

These are items of value, large or small. At the top end they
include your home (even if you are still buying it), pension, life
assurance policy and car. At the other end they include any items

of jewellery, pictures or antiques you may own, even things like
the stamp album in the attic and the old vase you would take to
the *Antiques Road Show* if it came to your area.

To find out what your assets are, separate out what is yours
from what is your husband or partner's and from what belongs to
other family members and/or dependants. You may have joint
ownership of some major items; include them in your list, but
bear in mind that they are not your property exclusively. For
some items you will need to separate out the capital value in £s
from the annual income that the asset provides, also in £s.

Liabilities

These are your commitments. They range from the mortgage on
your home to the hire-purchase payments on the car or video, and
include anything you still have to pay on your last holiday and the
balance (after deposit) on any you have booked for the future.
Don't forget any bank overdraft or outstanding balances on credit
cards, and remember any goods bought on interest-free credit.
Rates/community charges, water rates and gas, electricity and
telephone bills also need to be taken into account. Are you
committed to any payments to charities, family members or
professional institutions? Are there outgoings such as school fees
looming? You could have costs for storing furniture or insuring
jewellery. It is very important to know just what you owe and to
whom.

Never forget that many liabilities involve regular interest payments as well as paying off the basic sum borrowed. This may
seem obvious, but it causes problems for some people.

Moneyplanner – Wealth check

Assets

Home (estimated value) – what it could sell for less what is still
owed on mortgage _____

Car – what it could be sold for _____

Savings – building society and bank accounts _____

         – surrender values of any relevant insurance policies __

         – government stocks, shares, unit trusts and other
securities _____

         – other forms of savings _____

Tangible assets (including items of value over, say, £200) _____
Jewellery and the like which could have a collectable value ____
Home contents (what you could sell them for, not what they
cost – it may be worth having antiques valued) _____
Other (including special insurances) _____

Total assets _____

Liabilities
Mortgage/loans outstanding _____
Hire-purchase and/or shop credit debts _____
Overdraft or bank loans _____
Other outstanding loans _____
Credit card balances to be paid off _____
Other debts _____

Total liabilities _____

Assets less liabilities reflect your total wealth. If your liabilities
are more than your assets, you need to consider carefully how you
would make repayments if you suffered a reduction in income, or
had a sudden unexpected bill to pay or an unforeseen situation to
make provision for.

Now look at your assets and recognize the purposes they fulfil
and the security they represent. Recognize, too, the extent to
which each helps you secure other desirable assets, such as your
home. Your income will be helping to secure your pension and to
add to your other resources. You will feel more secure about your
health if you have health insurance to reduce worries about
immediacy of treatment. Your happiness and satisfaction with
your lifestyle will be more complete if you have 'rainy day'
money, if you can afford a good holiday from time to time and if
you can pay for a wedding in the family or help children to buy
their own homes. You will feel more secure, too, if you have the
knowledge that you can help others if the need should arise, and
that you will be able to pass on something to your children in due
course.

You need, too, to consider the implications of taxes. You must
take account of your present position, but should also think about
your future position, taking into consideration increasing age and
possible future catastrophes (such as a stock market crash or
personal, husband or partner incapacity because of illness, etc.).

It follows that you may need to decide to change the proportions of some of your assets so that you are better served by your resources.

SAVINGS AND INVESTMENTS

Section 12 will discuss savings and investments in detail. In this section, we concentrate on what you have. Look at the savings and investments Moneyplanner and draw up your own list by using it as a guide.

MONEYPLANNER – savings and investments

National Savings Certificates – nos. and values _____
Yearly Plan – nos. and values _____
Post office savings accounts – nos. and current balances _____
Building society accounts – nos. and current balances _____
Save As You Earn schemes – nos. and values _____
Premium Bonds – nos. and values _____
High interest bank accounts – nos. and current balances _____

Stocks, shares, unit trusts

Date bought	Name and description	Number of stocks, shares, units	Certificate numbers	Cost

WHAT YOU NEED TO ALLOW FOR

Now you know what you have, we will look in detail at your needs. The next chart gives you basic guidelines. They are given in a commonly accepted order of priority but bear in mind that your personal situation may give you a different order of priority.

The need	What to look for

1. *Protection*

Who pays the bills if you are ill for a long time, and if you have dependants what will happen to them if you die suddenly? The state has a wide range of benefits, but they may be insufficient for you or your dependants to enjoy a good standard of living if you stop earning. The solutions to this problem are cheap and simple and involve insurance policies.

The first step, if you are in a **company pension scheme,** is to know what the benefits are. Then there is **permanent health insurance,** which gives a regular income if you are ill. **Term assurance** and **whole life assurance** (possibly more expensive) pay a lump sum if you die. **Family income benefit** pays your family a regular income if you die. Don't be confused by other sorts of insurance at this stage. What you are concerned with here is protection, not savings.

Some banks arrange loans to enable you to pay for insurance protection against sickness, accident, unemployment and death.

As a rule of thumb, you should try to have a year's income available as a lump sum in case you die unexpectedly. Think also of insuring your husband or partner's life, particularly if you have young children.

2. *Savings*
You are likely to need cash from time to time to pay for big items such as the deposit on a house, a new car or a holiday.

3. *A home*
You may choose to rent, but buying a house is a good way of saving and is encouraged by tax concessions.

When you have paid off the mortgage or loan on it you will own a valuable asset. Of course, owning a house is not without problems. You have to pay for repairs and to insure it, and you will have to sell it if you decide to move. Provision needs to be made for these costs as well.

Keep some short-term savings easily available in one or more of: a bank, a building society, national savings.

You can always get at those savings quickly. But make sure your money is earning satisfactory interest until you need it.

An increasing number of people are opting to buy, and there is a growing number of schemes for house purchase. You will be faced with having to make a decision about how to finance your purchase. That involves quite complicated sums, which depend on your income, the current rate of interest and your age. Banks and building societies are the main sources of finance.

Mortgages can be of either the **repayment** type or the **endowment** type; the latter is linked to a life assurance policy. There are a number of schemes to help the first-time buyer or the person buying an older property.

Don't just take the first house that you see. Shop around, ask questions and get out your calculator. Believe it or not, the lenders actually want to lend you money! Get a quotation from a number of sources, each on the same basis – amount, number of years, interest rate, insurance benefits, etc., so that they are all comparable.

4. *Wealth creation*

Reserves are longer term savings – for retirement, for your children's future or for a major project some years ahead. You should not embark on this until you have satisfied yourself that you have adequately covered the first three priorities. You must be prepared to keep on saving for several years and, in some cases, accept some ups and downs in market values to get the best return over the longer term.

The types of investment you will be looking at are: **life assurance policies** of the savings type, **endowment** or **unit linked.** For most of these you have to save for at least ten years. Don't forget to check on surrender values in case you need the money before maturity – it can be expensive to surrender in the early years.

Then there are **unit trusts,** which have no fixed term, but the longer you save, the better; and **shares and investment trust shares.** You will need advice about all these and you must remember that their values may go down as well as up with market values.

Finally, there are **pensions.** As well as the government schemes and any scheme you may have at work, there are a number of other schemes through which you can benefit. If you are self-employed you should look particularly carefully at this way of saving.

Recent legislation has changed the picture – read Section 14 to ensure you know how these may affect you.

We shall now look at your starting position with regard to money under four headings:

- Your need for basic protection
- Your housing requirements

- Starting to plan for retirement and old age
- Savings and wealth creation.

Take a look at this simple set of questions to find out where you stand. The letters direct you to the appropriate points in the text below.

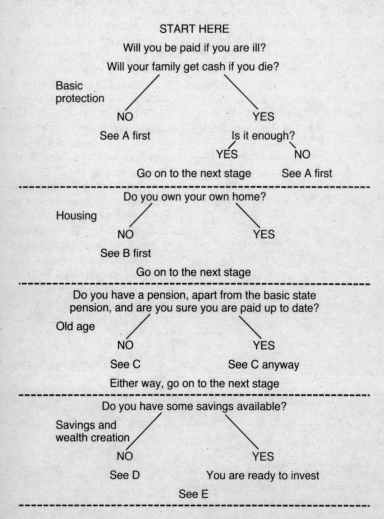

START HERE

Will you be paid if you are ill?

Will your family get cash if you die?

Basic protection

NO   YES

See A first   Is it enough?

YES   NO

Go on to the next stage   See A first

Do you own your own home?

Housing

NO   YES

See B first

Go on to the next stage

Do you have a pension, apart from the basic state pension, and are you sure you are paid up to date?

Old age

NO   YES

See C   See C anyway

Either way, go on to the next stage

Do you have some savings available?

Savings and wealth creation

NO   YES

See D   You are ready to invest

See E

Now look at all the implications.

A: Basic protection

If you fall sick and you are married, perhaps with a family, or if you die, who is going to pay the bills?

The ways to cover these situations are cheap and simple.

- *Term (or temporary) assurance.* This is just like whole-life assurance except that it lasts for a limited time (say ten or fifteen years). It is cheaper than whole-life assurance and well worth considering having while your family is growing up. It covers you within the term specified if you die, but you get nothing at the end. Your family, hopefully, will not need the support then, because you have not died.
- *Whole life assurance.* This pays a guaranteed sum when you die. The premium you pay will be related to the sum guaranteed and to your age. It is worth starting young and topping up for inflation as time goes by.
- *Endowment assurance.* This helps you to save for the future and insures your life. You pay premiums for a fixed number of years. The policy pays out a capital sum if you die during this period, or at the end if you are still alive. Endowment policies can be without profits (you get the guaranteed capital sum) or with profits (you get the sum plus a share of the life assurance company's profits).
- *Permanent health insurance.* This pays out a weekly or monthly income if you fall ill. It is particularly relevant if you are self-employed.

Don't become confused with other sorts of insurance at this stage. If you want simple protection only there is no point in paying for extra benefits you don't need. You should aim for cover of at least 75 per cent of your annual income, less any invalidity benefit that may be available. This basic protection is less important if you are single or retired. See also Section 4.

B: Somewhere to live

Buying a house or flat makes a lot of sense. The government encourages home ownership by giving tax relief on mortgage interest. The main advantage is that you will end up with a valuable asset, quite apart from having the pleasure and security of owning the roof over your head.

- Start by saving with a bank or building society as soon as you can afford to. Then, when you have enough for a deposit and the other expenses, you can look for a home, knowing you have the basic wherewithal.
- Before buying think very carefully about what type of mortgage will suit you best. Consider the different types and the different amounts they cost. Try to get impartial advice from someone who doesn't just want to sell you his or her product.
- If you rent from a local council, enquire about facilities for tenants to purchase. This can sometimes be done on attractive terms. See also Section 11.

C: Old age

Pensions is a complicated subject and the need for them often seems to be a long way off. Many people find this a good excuse not to think about them. But pension funds have tax advantages and are a particularly good way of saving. The over 45s, in particular, should think hard about providing for their future. Pension funds are of three main types:

- The state pension arrangements, both basic and earnings related.
- Company, government and local government schemes for their employees.
- Self-employed retirement schemes and personal pension plans.

Look particularly carefully at Section 14. This outlines the current position on personal pensions.

If you are in a company scheme you can often make additional contributions. Ask your pensions or personnel department. Pensions, like life assurance, cost much less when begun early than when started late. All insurance benefits come from invested premiums and the income that accrues from those investments. The longer the insurance company has been investing your premiums, the more pension you will get for any given rate of premium payment.

D: Short-term savings

This is the money available both for emergencies and for large purchases. Keep it readily available. The right places for it are:

- Banks
- Building societies
- National savings.

Each has different schemes over various periods; your choice will depend on how much you want to save and for how long. You must take into account which scheme will give you the best rate of interest. The amount you save will be determined by your own needs and desires, but a typical sum is between £5,000 and £7,000. Make sure you get a good rate of interest – the best may be from a high interest cheque account in your bank, a high interest account in a building society or even a deposit account.

E: Wealth creation
If you still have some money left after dealing with the preceding categories, you should think about building up capital. You should already be doing this to some extent through buying your home and through your pension scheme. Remember, though, that you should not confuse wealth creation with short-term savings. The most profitable schemes run for several years; short-term encashment of these can carry a penalty. The following are all long-term schemes:

- Long-term saving through life assurance companies, endowment policies and unit-linked policies
- Unit trusts
- Stocks and shares (including investment trusts)
- National savings – certain schemes
- Government stocks.

This is a wide and complex field. You may need more advice than is given in this book. Section 12 gives some details.

YOU AND WORK
Let us now take a look at you in relation to your work. You will not be surprised to learn that whether or not you have a job you are at work! The chances are that if you are looking after a home and a family on a full-time basis your attitude is just as professional as it would be to a 9.00 a.m. to 5.00 p.m. job. Ensuring that you make it a little more professional could easily save you both time and money – and time is money, of course.

If you do have a paid job you should examine how you feel about it, considering whether it is satisfying and whether you are getting what you feel you should in terms of money in exchange for your time. Also consider the options for doing better. Answer the questions below to assess where you stand in your current job and whether alternatives may be attractive.

You and your job

1. Do you like it, find it satisfying?

2. Do you earn the fair rate for the job? Do you feel imposed upon?

3. Do you know about your rights at work, your responsibilities to your employer and your employer's responsibilities to you regarding:
   – your contract of employment?
   – your position if you are ill?
   – your maternity rights?
   – the situation if you want to return to your job after the birth of a baby?
   – holiday pay?
   – your pension position if you are working part-time? (Be especially careful if your employer is contracted out of the state pension scheme: your pension could be at risk. This is very important if you want to move from full-time to part-time work, even in the same company. See Section 14.)
   – what happens if you have to leave work because you are being made redundant, are unfairly sacked or reach retirement age?

You can get information and advice from your local Jobcentre or Citizen's Advice Bureau on these matters, and also from your local DHSS office.

Longer working life for a woman

As you come nearer to retirement age, you will become more aware that some women have to retire five years earlier than men. European Community law favours levelling up the retirement ages for women and men – a law should soon be in force which gives women the right to work until they are 65 if they wish.

If you are on low pay or unemployed

It may be possible for you to increase your income by claiming help from the state in the following ways.

- *Family Credit*. If you have children you can claim Family Credit if you (or your husband or partner) work at least twenty-four hours a week. What you will get will depend on how much you earn and other circumstances.

- *Income Support*. If you (or your husband or partner) do not work enough hours to get Family Credit, you may be able to claim Income Support instead. This is a benefit available to you if you do not have enough money to live on.

- *Other sources of help*. You may also be able to get help from the Social Fund. If you are unemployed, of course, you should find out if you are eligible for Unemployment Benefit.

- *Help with housing costs*. You may be able to get help under the Housing Benefit scheme. What you get will depend on your particular circumstances.

For more information consult your local DHSS office or Citizen's Advice Bureau.

THE IMPORTANCE OF BUDGETING

If you are like most other people, you will probably wonder from time to time where all your money has gone. You may feel that your income should be enough to get by on, but sometimes it seems that there is a gaping hole down which a lot of money goes without your noticing it.

The principles are the same whether there is a lot of money or a little, and what is a lot to some of us is a little to others. Attitudes vary as well. Some women may think things are getting a bit tight when their current account seems close to sliding into overdraft. Others feel they do not have enough means when they are right at the top of the credit limit on their cards and cannot buy anything at all.

How do you make sure your income is enough?

There is no short cut – you must have a budget. Then you will know how much money is coming in and where the money goes.

The starting-point is where the money goes now. From there you can decide where you would like it to go. Usually there is a difference! Look at the budget Moneyplanner illustrated here.

MONEYPLANNER – budget

Income
Earnings
   Income from employment _____
   Income from self-employed earnings (before tax) _____
   Pensions _____
   Interest and other income _____
   Income taxed at source (from building society and bank) ____
   Interest on deposit or high interest cheque accounts, government stock interest and company share dividends (after tax) __
   Income not taxed at source (such as Girobank interest and national savings) (before tax) _____
   Child Benefit and other state benefits, alimony or child maintenance payments _____
   Income from property (e.g. letting rooms or part of your house) _____

   Subtotal _____

	Planned	Actual
Total year's income	_____	_____

Expenditure

	Essential	Non-essential
Housing	Rent/mortgage _____	
	Rates/community charge _____	
	Ground rent _____	
	Water rates _____	
	Maintenance/repairs __	
	Home insurance _____ (building and contents)	
Energy	Gas/oil/solid fuel _____	
	Electricity _____	
	Repairs/servicing _____	

Food	Groceries/milk, etc. ___	Alcohol _____
	Lunches/school meals __	Eating out _____
Clothing	Basic clothes/shoes ____	Clothes/shoes _____
	Basic cleaning/repairs __	Cleaning/repairs _____
	Basic toiletries _____	Toiletries/cosmetics ____
Household	Cleaning repairs _____	Housewares/durables __
	Furniture/furnishings __	Telephone _____
		Garden _____
Travel	Travel to work/school __	
Work costs		Subscriptions to
		professional bodies,
Children's	Child-minding, nursery	etc. _____
costs	costs, etc _____	

Car expenses (is the car essential, useful or simply a pleasure?)
    Hire purchase or vehicle credit payments _____
    Insurance, road tax, MOT test _____
    Running costs, including servicing and garage, tyres,
    batteries _____
    Depreciation _____

	Essential	**Non-essential**
Holidays and		Holidays _____
hobbies		Hobbies _____
		TV and video – credit
		costs/rent, service and
		licence _____
		Films and processing __
		Others _____
Incidentals	Postage _____	Books/papers _____
	Christmas/birthdays __	Children/babysitting/
		outings _____
		Education _____
		Subscriptions _____
		Medical and veterinary
		expenses _____
		Costs of keeping pets,
		e.g. food _____
		Lump sum gifts _____
		Charities _____
		Others _____

Tax/financial Tax – on earnings and   Professional fees _____
               investments _____   Bank and credit card
               Tax – paid through   interest _____
               PAYE _____
               National insurance
               contributions _____
Savings   Pensions _____   Regular savings _____
                                              Life insurance _____
Emergen-   Reserve for
cies   contingencies _____
Other
               Planned   **Actual**
Subtotal
               Planned   **Actual**
Total year's
income   _____   _____
Total year's
expenditure _____   _____

Now go back to the beginning of the budget Moneyplanner, and use it to draw up a list of your own. Use the same time scale as that in which your money comes in: monthly, if you have a monthly salary cheque or housekeeping allowance; weekly, if your income comes each week.

First, note all the money coming into the home (under Income), and then make a note of the expenses (under Expenditure). You will note that for most categories of expenditure the Moneyplanner is divided into essential and non-essential groupings. This should make you stop and think – then you can decide whether or not a particular item is essential to you!

While you are doing this, remember that this is going to be your own budget. There won't be room in it to list every item of expenditure, but the broad headings should cover all the ways in which you spend your money and you can move them around to suit you. Consider how much of the non-essential spending is really worthwhile for you, and whether it is giving you what you really want. Adjust the items to suit you, and you will have your own budget. Then it will be up to you to keep to it.

Remember to consider the implications of inflation. We are now in a period of low inflation, but you should, when you plan ahead, make an allowance for inflation so that you are not caught out. When doing this be overgenerous. If inflation is running at, say, 4 per cent, allow 5 or 6 per cent. Then you should have a nice surprise at the end of the year. If inflation has started roaring ahead again, then at least you will have made some realistic provision for it, and you will be able to adjust your figures from then on.

It is as well, also, to remember that some costs rise faster than others, and some rise faster than the rate of inflation. Allow for this.

Ensure you check up on your position at least quarterly, if not monthly.

Involve the family

If you have a family, do involve them. It makes things much easier if individual members of the family know that they have to pull their weight too. Don't take a schoolmistressy attitude – make it fun. Give the family an incentive to become involved. It is important to talk about this subject, and to work at it, as a family. For too long money management has been a taboo subject; if you bring it out into the open you will probably find that members of the family will respond positively.

Look at the overall picture

When you have filled in your budget, step back and look at it. If the first set of figures for expenditure adds up to more than your income you are probably being cautiously realistic; if less, check that no items have been forgotten.

Adjust the figures up and down so that they do balance. This will show you where you have perhaps to pull in your belt, and (hopefully) where it is possible to let it out and to indulge yourself. But be realistic about where you can make savings; remember that some expenses are less flexible than others.

It is particularly important to keep a little in reserve for emergencies. You can plan quite easily for what you expect; the unexpected things are the problem.

If you really take the trouble to look at the financial facts you will be surprised at how much further you can make your money go.

THE KEY RELATIONSHIPS

Let us now look at the key relationships in effective money management. The chances are that you have already established these, but you should examine them and understand how they affect you.

First, consider yourself in relation to the money machine. Look at the illustration called 'You and the money machine'. It shows you at the centre of what looks like a wheel. The spokes represent your access to your bank, your solicitor, your accountant, those with whom you arrange savings and investments yourself and any financial adviser who helps you choose investments and may also buy and/or manage them for you. There can be complementary relationships as well: some of those with whom you are doing business can talk to each other on your behalf. Your situation is helped when they do this effectively, and you probably fare worse when they don't.

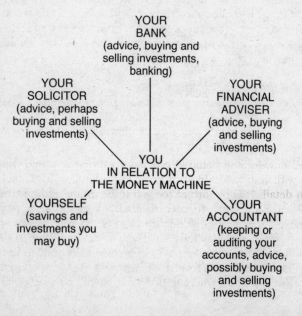

You and the money machine

YOUR
BANK
(advice, buying and
selling investments,
banking)

YOUR
SOLICITOR
(advice, perhaps
buying and selling
investments)

YOUR
FINANCIAL
ADVISER
(advice, buying
and selling
investments)

YOU
IN RELATION TO
THE MONEY MACHINE

YOURSELF
(savings and
investments you
may buy)

YOUR
ACCOUNTANT
(keeping or
auditing your
accounts, advice,
possibly buying
and selling
investments)

The second illustration, 'You and money products/services', makes the important point that you are really at the centre of a much larger wheel than the first one. The complete wheel takes in taxation, property, your will and other areas. Study this and, if you can, decide whether you are in a satisfactory position in all these areas.

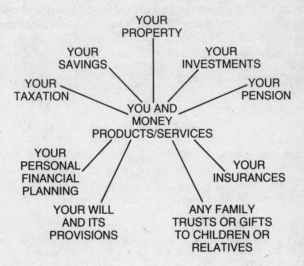

You and money products/services

We now look in detail at one key relationship which you have, that with your bank. In Section 12, this relationship will be looked at in detail. It is important for you to be aware of all instructions that you have given to your bank. Look at the bank payments Moneyplanner and draw one up to apply to you. If you are like most people, you may have to search about the home to find the information, but don't be put off – it is worth the effort. In future, keep all letters to and from your bank and other advisers in a safe place, so you know where to find them when you need them.

MONEYPLANNER – bank payments
Standing orders

Date due	Name of organization	Ref.	Amount	Last payment

Direct debits

Date started	Nature	Amount	Last payment

Always go over your bank statements to check that all payments in have been credited and that you have not been charged wrongly for payments out. It is also wise to check monthly balances and cash flows, to avoid overdrafts. If you can, try to ensure that you have free banking. Put any spare money into deposit accounts.

SUMMARY
- Find out where you stand in relation to your need for protection, saving and investment, and find out how well you understand how to relate money to your needs.
- Check up on your position with regard to work, if you have a job. Know where to turn if you need information.
- Check up on your own income and expenditure position.
- Take a serious and realistic attitude to budgeting.
- Identify those with whom you have key relationships with regard to money management.
- Above all, resolve to run your own financial affairs, instead of letting them run you.

Section 4

The need for insurance

INTRODUCTION

At the heart of good, effective personal money management is the need not to have nasty surprises.

Surprises can easily blow your financial ship off-course. One way to protect against them is by taking out insurance. This section will identify the different types of insurance you should consider when you are thinking about protection, and the key factors within them.

Insurance for protection is, of course, a large and important subject. In this book I try to signpost the priorities for you as a woman. Sources of information and help are also identified in Appendix 8.

Look now at the insurance Moneyplanner – it will help to show you whether you have been making the necessary provisions. Most people tend to get confused about insurance; this list gives details of the different types which you should consider, ranging from home to holiday. Not all types are necessarily relevant to you but a quick look at the headings will help you see if you have forgotten any relevant areas. Draw up your own list, even though it will take time. You will find that you have a valuable record when it is complete, and you can update it from time to time, as necessary.

MONEYPLANNER – insurance

Home buildings (the structure of your flat, maisonette, house, etc.)
Company _____
Policy no. _____
Amount covered and conditions _____
Premium _____
Date due _____

(Check what the landlord insures for if you do not own your house freehold.)

House contents and personal effects
Company _____
Policy no. _____
Amount covered and conditions _____
Premium _____
Date due _____
(Check if the policy includes public liability cover and all risks on valuable items such as cameras and jewellery.)

Mortgage protection
Company _____
Policy no. _____
Amount covered and conditions _____
Premium _____
Date due _____
Date policy comes to an end _____

Car
Company _____
Policy no. _____
Type, amount covered and conditions _____
Premium _____
Date due _____

Life assurance – term and/or whole life
Company _____
Policy no. _____
Dated _____
Sum assured and conditions _____
Maturity date _____
Premium _____
Date due _____

Life assurance – endowment (savings)
Company _____
Policy no. _____
Dated _____
Sum assured and conditions _____
Maturity date _____
Premium _____
Date due _____

Family income
Company _____
Policy no. _____
Amount covered and conditions _____
Premium _____
Date due _____

Pensions – personal/company
Company _____
Policy no. _____
Amount covered and conditions _____
Premium _____
Date due _____

Personal accident/health insurance
Company _____
Policy no. _____
Amount covered and conditions _____
Premium _____
Date due _____

Holiday
Company _____
Policy no. _____
Amount covered and conditions _____
Premium _____
Date due _____

Others (Consider whether you should have a policy to cover a pet.
Remember that the film star Betty Grable even insured her legs.)
Nature/type _____
Company _____
Policy no. _____
Amount covered and conditions _____
Premium _____
Date due _____

What conclusions can you draw? Do you have too little insurance cover or too much? Is there any duplication? Could you get
schemes to suit you better? Will they be cheaper? What about
looking at the schemes on offer from organizations such as the
AA and the RAC, to which you may belong? Will membership
give you good insurance at a cheaper rate? Remember that credit

cards frequently include some insurance cover, particularly for travel, holiday or business. Check that you know your own position.

KNOW WHERE YOU STAND ON INSURANCE

Until recent years the man in a family was traditionally regarded as the one responsible for insurance as he was bread-winner, home-owner, keeper of the family purse, etc. If anything happened to the man, the woman tended to take over responsibility for insurance cover on house, contents, children and so on without giving a second thought about its suitability

As a woman, you now very definitely need to make – or share in – decisions on insurance matters. This is for several different reasons, including the following:

- You may be the head of the household.
- You may be left to raise and educate children if anything happens to your husband or partner.
- You are the likely inheritor of substantial assets on your husband's or partner's death, and need to consider inheritance tax liability when these pass to your children or other relatives.
- You may be the key person in a business.
- You may be a car-owner.
- You are a possible heir to relations, and a possible winner of cash prizes, from bingo, football pools, etc.

Insurance is making provision against the worst eventualities. If you face up to statistical facts, you will recognize that it is much less likely that your home will be burned to the ground during the next ten years than that you may die. We all insure against our premature death grudgingly if at all, while accepting without question the need for a hefty buildings insurance policy. Women's lives are often grossly underinsured, especially in the case of young mothers at home bringing up children. For many families, a young mother's premature death would involve either employing help in the house or the husband or partner having to reduce or give up his job to look after the children.

LIFE ASSURANCE
You need to look at the subject of life assurance both from the point of view of yourself (the insured) and the insurer (the insurance company).

- You will wish to insure your own life to help your family or dependants if you die early.
- You need to insure your husband's or partner's life in order to provide a capital sum for home maintenance, family responsibilities, etc., in case of his death.
- You may need to insure for school fees, child care, etc., in case your husband or partner dies first and you cannot work. (Look at the possibility of a joint life and survivor policy with your husband or partner.) In case you die first you need to have insurance so that your husband or partner can provide for the children while he continues to work.
- With present high property values there is an increasing risk of a heavy inheritance tax bill if you die after your husband or partner and the estate goes to children or other relatives. You may need to be covered to avoid your property being sold over the heads of your children.
- You need to insure for loss of your husband's or partner's earnings if he is sick for a long time. You should also consider the advantage of writing life policies in trust, under the terms of the Married Women's Property Act of 1882, in favour of named beneficiaries rather than of the estate. This has benefits in terms of providing:
  – instant money
  – few formalities.
It also avoids having the sum paid out included with the remainder of the estate for inheritance tax purposes.

Meanings of insurance terms
Insurance terms used to be difficult to understand and technical terms abounded in policy prospectuses letters, and other documents. The paperwork is now becoming easier to understand. In the glossary (Appendix 7) you will find explanations of the terms most often used.

Life assurance – the income tax position
If you are paying premiums on life assurance policies taken out before the March 1984 Budget, you are getting income tax relief on the annual premiums. From March 1984 this tax relief has been abolished on new policies taken out but, even so, a with-profits endowment policy represents a good way of saving, especially for a younger woman, for whom premiums are low.

INSURANCE AND HEALTH

Now that women are playing increasingly important roles in business and in the home, it is important to minimize periods of incapacity through illness.

You should consider a health care plan if you are not already covered by your husband's or partner's, or by an employer's scheme. This will meet medical costs and enable prompt attention to be given to your medical condition if you need it. There are many medical treatment insurance schemes run by private health organizations, of which BUPA and PPP are the best known. You can also get plans which give cover for specific medical needs, such as hip replacement. Then there are permanent health insurances that provide a regular income if you become incapacitated.

If you have a job, check your position and, if necessary, try to encourage your employer to enter into a group health scheme. This will give you the benefit of cheaper and more immediate treatment. If your employer pays the premiums, though, they will be taxable as a benefit arising from your employment.

Property and contents of your home

Homes are all too often underinsured, so do check up on your position. If you are underinsured, an insurance company may only pay out *pro rata* on any claim you make. You could lose out badly as a result. You need to do your own inventory, putting replacement costs or values against everything, and then add them all up.

If you are a property-owner you should ignore the market value of your home and have it covered for full replacement value – to include full rebuilding costs, legal and architect's fees and also the cost of living somewhere else during rebuilding. The amount can be calculated, based on a rate per square metre of area – annual suggested figures are available from the Royal Institution of Chartered Surveyors and the Association of British Insurers. They vary according to locality. This information can also be found in the Association of British Insurers' leaflet, *Buildings Insurance*.

Do make sure your policy includes, in addition to the standard risks, flooding, subsidence, vehicle impact, storm damage, etc.

Once you have arrived at the correct base figure, you should get your policy index-linked to ensure the cover is adequately increased year by year.

You should insure the contents of your home, if you can, for full replacement value. It is worth considering 'new for old'; otherwise a deduction for wear and tear will be made from any claim and you could be in for a nasty surprise. Index-linking is also important to ensure you don't lose out if inflation rises. It is important, too, to remember to raise the sum insured to cover any new items acquired – hi-fi equipment, a new and more expensive washing-machine, a new freezer, etc.

Remember to look out for discounts offered by your insurance company, such as when burglar alarms, special locks or smoke detectors are fitted. Also check that your policy includes third-party liability in case someone brings a claim against you.

You may need a special all risks policy for your valuables, such as jewellery, pictures, etc. Make sure that anything valuable which you take outside the home regularly is fully covered.

MORTGAGE PROTECTION

Whenever you enter into a mortgage jointly with a partner or in your own right, you should take out insurance cover for the outstanding balance of the mortgage in order to provide funds to repay it in the event of death. This is relatively cheap. Some policies include a small inbuilt life-cover provision; others don't, so watch out! There are many alternatives to choose from, including some life policies; shop around for the best value for your money.

Mortgages are often linked with insurance policies for the payment of premiums; see Section 11 for details.

INSURANCE AND THE CAR

Shop around for the best deal for you. Do remember that cheapest isn't always best! You need security of cover and a prompt service if you make a claim. There is a higher likelihood of a claim on a motor policy than on most other insurance policies. You will need to choose a policy which states what it covers: one driver, named drivers only or any driver. Clearly the rates offered will vary accordingly. If you choose to be the only driver, look out for special discounts for women – many companies offer them.

The basic legal requirement is for third-party insurance only. For a cheap, older car, third-party, fire and theft cover may be adequate, but, if you can afford it, it is always wise to opt for comprehensive car insurance. If you have an older car which is increasing in value or becoming the subject of a cult, do watch that you are not underinsured and that there are no awkward clauses about spare parts. There are special rates and special policies for interesting old vehicles.

Remember that premiums will vary with the type of car, the cover required and the area in which you live. Remember too that you may need insurance for using your car for business purposes. Also, it is wise, if you can, to insure against legal expenses in relation to a possible future motor accident and possible claims against you related to motoring.

No claims discount is a valuable asset; it pays to be a careful driver with a clean driving licence. The discount can save you a lot of money, particularly if you live in a big city. For a small additional premium it is possible to insure the discount so that you do not lose it if you make a claim. There are certain conditions attached: for example, you may be able to make two claims in three years only without affecting your discount.

It is important to keep your car insurance policy in a safe place, and also to keep a separate record of the details. You will be issued with an insurance certificate. Keep it with you, alongside your driving licence, when driving, in case of an accident. You will need to produce it when you renew your car tax.

TRAVEL INSURANCE

If you travel regularly or are about to undertake a long journey, think about travel insurance. What should you cover?

The first thing to do is to cover yourself – against injury or death by accident. Remember that if you pay for your travel with certain credit cards you are automatically given insurance cover. Also, you can sometimes obtain temporary cover at the start of a journey by buying an insurance voucher at the airport or at the station when you get your ticket. For fuller cover you need to look for a specific policy from an insurance company.

A word of advice about your luggage: do check whether it is covered properly. Your home contents policy may cover it, but it may not. The extent of the cover on your luggage may depend on your means of travel – the position may differ according to whether the luggage is on a ship or an aircraft, for instance. Don't underinsure; clothes and personal belongings are expensive to replace! Remember also the cost of suitcases themselves.

It almost goes without saying that you need to insure against loss of money or theft, if you are taking large sums of money about with you. There are also schemes for registering and insuring keys and credit cards – if they go missing only one telephone call to the relevant organization is necessary; they will do everything needed to safeguard you from the effects of misuse.

If you are not in such a scheme, always carry with you a note of your card numbers and the address and telephone numbers of the issuers so that you can report any loss at once. Most insurers will only undertake to protect you from misuse of your cards if you notify them of their loss within a stated period. Make sure you know what this period is so that you don't do too little, too late.

You should also consider covering yourself against the cost of medical treatment abroad, which can be alarmingly expensive, and also against the cost of returning home in case you cannot do that in the way you intended. Car repatriation can also be covered. There are many schemes available for these.

HOLIDAY INSURANCE
All of what has been said under travel insurance applies also to holidays.

Holiday insurance is often included in the price of a package holiday or offered as an optional extra. It is generally very well worth having. One valuable part of the package is cover against your having to cancel the holiday, e.g. through illness. If a family member is ill and you can't go away, you could find yourself paying in full for a holiday you never had.

There may also be cover against your being involved in a lot of hassle, delay and extra expense because of a strike by one of the essential services, which is, alas, a frequent hazard these days.

BUSINESS INSURANCE
If you have a key role in a business – as an executive or partner – or are self-employed, you should be aware of the extra insurance needs which these responsibilities bring. The following are some of the areas to be considered.

Business cover
In addition to covering the business premises and contents, just as

you would your own home, you need to think of your responsibilities to your staff, your customers and the public. You must by law have employer's liability cover, and public liability insurance will cover you in the event of a claim being made against you by members of the public.

Depending on the nature of your business, you may also need product liability insurance to cover you against claims made against you regarding the things you produce or the services you sell. You may also need professional indemnity insurance to cover you if someone makes a claim against you because they suffered loss or damage as the result of advice you gave them.

Key person insurance
If you are a key person in your business, severe disruption and financial loss could result if anything happened to keep you away from work for a lengthy period of time. You can insure against this.

Loss of profits
Your business could suffer loss of work or production, resulting in loss of profits and financial hardship, if, for example, the business premises were damaged or destroyed. A loss-of-profits policy (also called business interruption) will cover you against this event.

Specialist information
Business insurance is a complex field and the cover required varies very much according to each individual business situation. If you need business insurance you should seek the help and advice of an insurance broker with specialist knowledge. They will be able to suggest a suitable insurance package for your needs. The Association of British Insurers offers a free package called 'Small Business Insurance Advice Files'. If you would like one, write to them direct, you will find their address in Appendix 4.

INSURANCE ON CREDIT AND BORROWING
No survey of insurance for women would be complete without mentioning the insurance cover offered when you take out a loan or commit yourself to a large hire-purchase or credit-sale transaction.

Consumer credit has reached new heights with the recent boom in spending, bringing with it an inevitable increase in the number of those who find themelves in serious financial difficulty because of misfortunes such as redundancy, illness, family break-up and so on. Repayments which seemed easy to maintain while everything was going well suddenly become impossible when they are going less well.

Even if you cannot foresee ever being afflicted by misfortunes that could affect your financial situation, you should consider taking out insurance cover so that the repayments can be continued if you are unable to make them. But here is a word of warning: check very carefully the exact extent of any insurance cover you are offered, and make sure you know where you stand. In many cases insurance cover will last only for six months following loss of earnings through redundancy. This gives you some breathing space but at the end of that period you will be on your own again.

WHAT IF THINGS GO WRONG?
If you need help and advice, where do you turn? There are many organizations which are able to offer information and advice and some can help in practical ways as well. In the appendices you will find details.

SUMMARY
- Always shop around for insurance. Don't be guided by price alone; also consider what cover you need and what is offered.
- Make sure, every year, that you are not underinsured.
- Make sure you understand what is not covered.
- Look at whether you need a policy in relation to the Married Woman's Property Act (see Section 9).
- Do be sure you disclose all relevant facts, including any changes. Telling the company (or broker) anything and everything that could be relevant is an essential component of all contracts for insurance – called, legally, *uberrimae fides* (utmost faith).
- Keep clearly in mind the difference between positive and negative insurance. Don't assume that because something is not mentioned, it is covered.

Section 5

Using credit and coping with borrowing and repayments

This section is aimed at helping you clear your mind about the emotive subject of borrowing money.

It offers a checklist of all the different ways now open to almost all of us to obtain credit; reminds you of some pitfalls to avoid; and helps you make the best decisions for yourself when you are considering taking a loan.

The same principles can be applied to all forms of credit and borrowing. Most of them are dealt with here. The biggest loan of all for most of us, for a house, is dealt with in Section 11.

This section deals with:

- Using credit and coping with borrowing and repayments
- The price of borrowing
- The warning signs in relation to credit and debt
- Credit vetting
- Bank credit cards and store cards
- Banks and building societies in relation to credit
- Other sources of credit.

THE BACKGROUND TO THE PRESENT SITUATION

A few decades ago the word 'credit' was often used in a complimentary way; someone who was creditworthy was in good standing, a pillar of society with good resources who could be trusted to handle money well. They could safely be lent money. When credit cards were introduced, they were issued to people in this category, who would pay their accounts on receipt.

Credit cards grew in popularity and, for many people, became a regular means of borrowing money temporarily. The result is that now 'credit' means 'borrowing'. The term 'charge card' is used for cards issued under the same terms as the original credit card; accounts for charge cards are paid straightaway and there is no means of borrowing money by delaying payments.

ATTITUDES TOWARDS BORROWING

Many of us were brought up to believe that it was wrong, or at least foolish, to lend or borrow money at all. In medieval times there were strong social and economic arguments against usury. The Church was opposed to it. Shakespeare, in Polonius' advice to his son in *Hamlet,* advised 'Neither a borrower nor a lender be'. The same attitude underpinned the Victorians' strong disapproval of debt. Some religions in modern times prohibit usury.

Since World War II, though, three things have happened which have modified those traditional attitudes. First, the bulk of the population has become customers of banks and other providers of financial services and obtained access to consumer credit. The resulting boom in credit has, in successive reviews and reports, been judged as a general social good, contributing to the rise in our standard of living. Millions have benefited from car ownership and holidays, television sets and washing-machines because they have been able to borrow.

Secondly, in periods of high inflation it has been sound financial practice to borrow at today's prices as it will be easy to repay from tomorrow's inflated wages, avoiding paying tomorrow's inflated prices. This further inflates prices and increases interest rates, so it is not necessarily as good a strategy as it may appear to be.

Thirdly, more and more people need to use credit facilities to get by in today's world. For instance, the lack of, or overloading of, public transport in some areas makes private transport an essential means of travel to work for many. In buying a car by hire purchase or with a loan, we are changing from paying as we go (so much a journey, a week or a year for bus or train fares) to buying several years' journeys in advance, and we can do that without saving the capital sum to buy a car for cash.

CREDIT AND BORROWING AS FACTS OF LIFE

During 1987 Britain's consumers increased their outstanding debts by 18 per cent, so that by the end of the year they collectively owed £36·4 billion, quite apart from mortgages on houses and flats. The figure covers credit agreements with banks, building societies and finance companies and borrowing by credit cards.

The rise in serious debt problems is a cause for real concern. During the 1980s it became the single largest category of problem brought to Citizen's Advice Bureaux. Fortunately, the vast majority of credit arrangements and loan repayments are successfully managed. However, for those who get it wrong there can be many problems. Some of them are outlined in this book, along with suggestions for avoiding them. This section aims to help you stay with the majority and guard against overcommitment, which can combine with an unforeseen drop in income to turn using credit into coping with debt.

The price of borrowing

Make sure you have weighed up the pros and cons of paying more for something by borrowing in order to have it immediately. That extra cost is still high in the UK, despite the massive growth in the credit industry. There are, however, encouraging signs that some organizations have seen the advantages of lending to the consumer at more modest interest rates. Others may follow.

Go into it with your eyes open

We are now used to comparing the cost of different brands of food and, when such matters as the packaging and weights vary, looking for prices per kilo in order to compare like with like. We need to make comparisons between different credit packages in just the same ways. All lenders must, by law, advertise the annual percentage rate (APR) on their loans. You don't need to understand how the APR is calculated; simply be aware that it enables you to compare different credit offers. The lower the APR figure, the lower the cost of borrowing.

Don't worry if you had difficulty with percentages at school. The add-on cost percentage figure need only be thought of as extra pence to be paid on top of each £ borrowed. £1 borrowed at 27 per cent APR and repaid one year later means that you will have to repay £1 and then find, in addition, an extra 27p, i.e. £1.27 in total. For £100 borrowed at 27 per cent APR you would repay £127 at the end of the year.

Don't just look at the monthly repayment figure

Never make a decision to take on a credit or hire-purchase

agreement simply because the monthly repayment figure looks manageable.

You need to find out four things in addition to the monthly payments. These are:

- The APR – the lower the better
- How long the loan goes on for
- What the total you have to pay back is
- How much interest, in total, you have to pay.

As an example, you may want to borrow £3,000, and you may think that a bank personal loan is the best way to do it. You are offered two schemes: £75 per month for five years, and £275 per month for one year. A monthly payment of £75 (APR 18·7 per cent) is obviously easier to manage than a monthly payment of £275 (APR 19·5 per cent). But remember that the £75 per month repayment is for sixty months (five years); at the end of the loan you would have paid back a total of £4,500, of which £1,500 would be interest. By contrast, at £275 a month for twelve months (one year), you would pay back £3,300, of which only £300 would be interest.

This may seem obvious, but unfortunately it isn't always so easy to be aware of such differences when you are actually deciding how best to buy something you have set your heart on.

How long you should borrow for can depend on why you are borrowing. If the loan is for a holiday, and you will want another one next year, a twelve-month term is best. If you want to change your car every two years, it will make sense to have a two-year loan. On the other hand, if you want a new kitchen or furniture which will have a long life, a five-year term might be right, provided you are short of income and prepared to pay the extra interest costs that go with the longer term loan.

To give another example, if £3,000 was wanted for a newer car, a two-year loan with an APR of 19·7 per cent and £150 a month repayments would be right for the purpose. The total interest paid would be £600, whereas you would pay £300 for a one-year loan and £1,500 for a five-year loan.

Shop around
When you are sure you have your eyes wide open on the real cost of borrowing, you can not only judge whether something is worth buying through credit, but you can also choose the best credit deal

for what you need. The booklet, *Shopping Around for Credit,* issued by the Office of Fair Trading, will help you.

Interest-free credit

It is always worth bearing in mind the situations in which credit is free:

- Special offers from shops of 0 per cent (provided the cost of lending isn't recouped in a higher price)
- Credit-free periods following credit card purchases (but not cash withdrawals), gained by settling before the monthly due date
- Goods on account, where payment is to be settled by the end of the following month
- Goods bought on a charge card (always to be settled monthly).

Keep it under control

With a one-off loan, with equal repayments over a set period, you know what commitment you are taking on. The monthly credit card facility, the most commonly used form of credit, needs to be watched more carefully. The charges on any amount overdue, shown on your statement as a monthly interest figure, don't look at all alarming. But many people discover that if they pay off less each month than they have in fact spent since their previous statement, their debt increases month by month. In a frighteningly short time they can drift into the beginnings of serious debt problems.

People are in general now more careful with their credit cards than they used to be, tending to take advantage of the free credit period by paying by the monthly due date. Almost a half of Access and Visa card-holders discipline themselves regularly to do this.

For many people, handling one credit card is manageable, but a bundle of cards can be much more difficult. Provided you are considered basically creditworthy (for example, by having an apparently secure job and a bank account with a cheque guarantee card), you will find many would-be lenders happy to offer you credit. A wallet full of credit and store cards can lead to matters sliding dangerously out of control.

Beware of the automatic raising of the borrowing limit on your credit card; it can seem flattering when a letter to that effect arrives from the card company. Then there are unsolicited offers of more credit cards and higher borrowing limits. The onus is on you to set the limits on what you can handle – it's your money.

Different types of card are being introduced constantly. These include 'smart' cards (with memories), debit cards (you pay for the goods the instant you buy them, the money being taken from your bank account automatically) and new types of charge cards (confirming you as a creditworthy customer).

Your priorities
You can assess with confidence how much you can safely set aside for borrowing repayments – and therefore how much you can afford to borrow – if you consider it within a complete personal or family budgeting exercise.

Drifting into a bank overdraft on your current account is far more expensive than many people realize. An agreed overdraft facility, arranged beforehand with your bank, can be among the cheapest forms of credit, but going into the red can result in the bank charging you a much higher rate of interest. Remember too that you will lose out on free banking if you have an overdraft. Always discuss any possible need for overdraft with your bank first – it will help them to handle your account without embarrassing you, it will add to their confidence in you and it will also save you money.

STOP AND THINK
The single most important message is that you must stop and think, both about whether to borrow and about how much and for how long. This will help you avoid getting into serious debt problems.

Weigh up the need to borrow against waiting until you can afford to pay cash; compare the advantage of having something now against the cost of using consumer credit. It is especially important to stop and think when something you want is made easily available through instant credit offered in High Street shops.

Consider paying a bit extra and obtaining credit insurances to protect you against unforeseen change of circumstances and inability to keep up your repayments.

WATCH FOR THE WARNING SIGNS

Watch out for the danger signals which warn you that you may be heading for trouble.

- *Credit limits*. You have too many small debts – in different places. Your credit card accounts, bank overdraft and store credit are all at their limits.
- *Delays ahead*. You find you are asking for more and longer term credit, and stretching the time limits on all your bills.
- *Diversion*. You find it more and more difficult to talk to anyone about money. If you have a bank account, you cannot face the manager.
- *Last post*. You are scared to read letters – especially letters in window envelopes!

It is obviously wise to avoid all these, but if the symptoms do occur, then deal with things right away. Never put things off, hoping the troubles will go away. They won't; they will probably become worse.

BEWARE OF THE WOLF IN SHEEP'S CLOTHING

A secured loan can be one wolf. Some people imagine that this expression means that the loan is in some way safer for you, the borrower. It can be just the opposite. The lender is inviting you to risk losing the roof over your head to make sure he can get his money back if you fail to keep up your regular repayments. He can take you to court, making a claim on the proceeds from a sale of your assets – notably your home. Be very sure that you can meet the repayments before offering your house or flat as security for a loan.

Then there are loans for paying off other debts. These are often referred to as consolidation loans. Although they may offer the apparent immediate advantage of paying off several awkward debts, replacing them with a single regular repayment, if you take one on you may well be exchanging several unsecured loans for a new loan with your home as security (many advertisements say 'Only home-owners eligible' or 'Sorry, no tenants'). Only take this type of loan on if you are absolutely sure you can meet all the repayments on time.

Remember that banks offer secured loans. You should talk to

your bank before committing yourself to any home-owners loan advertised in the press. Compare the terms of various types and be sure you get the best deal.

CREDIT VETTING

Have you had trouble in obtaining credit? There may be a black mark against your name (perhaps mistakenly) in a computer data bank somewhere. The personal details you provide when applying for credit will be subjected to the process of credit scoring and checked out with a credit reference agency. If you feel you are being unreasonably denied access to credit facilities, you have the right to see what is entered against your name by a credit reference agency and to have any false statements corrected.

The more responsible the lenders, the more they will be concerned not to grant credit to people unlikely to be able to meet their side of the agreement.

Conversely, the more eager the lender is to offer instant credit, the more important it is for you to be sure you are not over-stretching yourself with borrowing commitments.

FORMS OF BORROWING

Here is a checklist of some of the different forms of borrowing.

Bank credit cards

Examples are Access and Visa.
- Limit set to total credit allowed
- No interest if settled in full by the specified date following the date of the statement
- Minimum monthly repayment of £5 or 5 per cent (whichever is the larger) of the amount due
- Interest on credit outstanding expressed as a percentage figure for the month
- Can be used very widely in the UK and overseas
- There may be automatic insurance when used to buy travel
- The Consumer Credit Act offers some fall-back protection if the suppliers of the goods or services fail.

Charge cards and gold cards

These are offered by some bank and credit card organizations, e.g. Diners and American Express.

- Joining and annual fees are usual; it is a privilege to be accepted
- Extended credit not offered; accounts must be settled monthly
- No limit to the spending which can be run up each month
- No Consumer Credit Act fall-back protection
- Increasing number of member privileges being developed, such as insurances
- Automatic bank overdraft facility offered in some cases, at advantageous interest rates.

Airline cards, hotel cards and others
Examples are Air Plus, Hertz, Avis and Trumpcard.
- Basically charge cards
- Usually special advantages for booking journeys, cars, hotel rooms, etc.
- There may be extras such as insurance
- Can save time on arrival or departure.

Store cards
Examples are John Lewis, Harrods and Marks & Spencer. Various types are offered by different stores and chains.
- Most work like credit cards – you buy at the store without cash and pay on receipt of statements.
- You may agree to pay a fixed sum each month, and can then acquire goods up to a set limit – perhaps twenty times your monthly payment.
- Interest rates range from just below those of the bank credit cards to rather higher than them.
- They are restricted to use in a single store or chain of shops.
- Member privileges are being developed, such as special late shopping evenings and previews of new fashions.

Other methods of borrowing
In addition to the ways of borrowing shown in the checklist, there are various other ways.

Personal loans from banks and building societies
These are agreed sums made available by a bank or building society, to be repaid over an agreed time. The means of repayment will be discussed, and security or collateral will sometimes

(not often) be required. Usually the interest rate is fixed at the outset, which can help you budget.

Flexible loan accounts
These are offered by banks and are similar to many store cards. You agree to pay a fixed sum each month, and can borrow from the account (up to an agreed multiple of the monthly payment figure), paying appropriate interest. The interest rates on these accounts vary from time to time.

Bank overdraft
A bank overdraft is often worth asking for as an alternative to a personal loan or borrowing on a credit card. The traditional overdraft can limit payment of interest to the days in the month on which you are in overdraft, and the interest rate charged will be amongst the lowest available. Beware, though; you may have to pay bank charges for three months, even if the overdraft is only for a few days.

Credit unions
These offer an extremely cheap form of borrowing. You must be eligible to join an existing union or to be involved in setting one up. A credit union is a mutual self-help society, whose members must share commitment through a common bond – examples are living on a particular estate, working for the same company, and being members of a certain church or of a work association. Members are effectively their own bank; they can obtain low interest rates if the credit union members accept that they do not want dividends to cover their risks and outgoings – or are willing to forego the usual level of interest on their money when they lend it to the union.

The drawback is that the credit union depends on members' savings to fund the loans. To maintain low interest for borrowings, savings can only attract low interest, also the size of loans is usually limited. The advantage is that no security is normally required because members trust each other.

Finance house loans
These are replacing traditional hire purchase. The finance company simply lends you the money without any complications of

itself owning the goods and having to reclaim them if you cannot keep up your payments. But the goods may still be forfeited if you do not keep up the payments.

Hire purchase

This is always worth comparing with other forms of credit, because it may be cheaper (although sometimes it is more expensive). Your initial deposit and monthly instalments cover the cost of the goods and interest payments.

The disadvantage is that the goods are not yours until the final payment has been made, and they can be repossessed if you fail to keep up your instalments. You will need to see if you have to make arrangements to insure the goods. Also, if you buy a car by hire purchase, you may be responsible for properly maintaining it and repairing it if there is an accident. In addition, of course, you cannot sell the goods until they have been fully paid for.

SUMMARY

- Borrowing is easy, but it costs you money.
- There are many pitfalls – look out for them.
- Set the costs (and disadvantages) of borrowing against the advantages of having the goods or services before you can pay for them.
- Shop around and choose the system that will suit you best for each type of borrowing.
- Ensure that credit arrangements are part of your personal financial plan so that problems do not creep up on you unexpectedly.

Section 6

You and your tax

INTRODUCTION

For most of us, the less we have to do with the tax office, the better we like it. But we have to live with tax, so it is worth trying to get it right.

Income tax – the very words conjure up visions of complicated forms, full of figures and words we don't understand, and a lot of time and effort spent. The outcome of filling in the forms, more often than not, is that we understand little more about where we stand than we did when we started.

For most of us our tax objectives are the same:

- We want to arrange our affairs so as to be liable for as little tax as possible.

- We want to be sure we are not paying more tax than we should.

- We want it all to be as simple, painless, easy and quick as possible.

This section, therefore, takes a look at the complex matter of income and other taxes with these objectives in view. Do note, however, that tax laws change from year to year, so you must make sure you have the latest information.

The section aims to:

- Put you in the picture with regard to income and other taxes

- Give you some essential information

- Show you how you may be able to pay less tax

- Deal with particular opportunities and problems for women.

TAX – THE ESSENTIALS

Income tax

You may understandably be confused when you receive various notices from different branches of the Inland Revenue.

First, there are inspectors of taxes who study your income as shown on the income tax returns you fill in. They assess what tax you should pay, and deal with any resultant problems. They tell the collectors of taxes how much they should get from you. Then there are collectors of taxes, who collect taxes and send out demands for arrears. Things can be particularly confusing if your tax assessments or collections are dealt with by more than one office.

There is a silver lining to the income tax cloud – the Inland Revenue is getting much better at understanding the problems they cause you. If you have questions about income tax, go and enquire personally at your nearest tax office. Remember to take the relevant information: a copy of the form you filled in, your last assessment and notice of coding, any reference number they have used on information they have sent to you and, ideally, also your national insurance number. Have all the necessary details and correspondence ready in case it is needed. Telephone before you go to the office, so that they can have all their files ready.

Your income tax is assessed on the income you receive in a tax or fiscal year (which runs from 6 April of one year to 5 April of the next). Your income includes payments you receive for work and unearned income from investments, savings and any other benefits. Remember that you have to declare income that is already taxed, such as interest from a bank or building society. You must also declare any income from a pension or from letting property, including letting a room in your own house.

It is possible to claim certain allowances. These reduce your tax bill. Everybody who is earning gets a personal allowance. The married man's personal allowance is a deduction against the aggregate income of husband and wife. There is an additional allowance against the earned income of the wife. You will also get tax relief on certain outgoings – for example, on mortgage payments for your home. There are many allowances, such as on subscriptions to professional and qualifying bodies that give you credentials for doing your job.

Tax is charged on your taxable income – the amount left after your allowances and certain outgoings have been subtracted from your total or gross income. It is also charged on benefits you may have as part of your employment. There are special rules covering cars and taking your husband on business trips, when the costs are paid by your employer.

Income tax, since the 1988 Budget
The current position with regard to allowances is as follows:

Single person's and wife's earned income	£2,605
(if a wife's earnings are less, the allowance is equal to her earnings)	
Married man's earned income	£4,095
Additional allowance for one-parent families and widow's bereavement	£1,490
Single person's (age 65–79)	£3,180
Married man's (age 65–79);	£5,035
Single person's (age 80+)	£3,310
Married man's (age 80+)	£5,205
Age allowance income limit	£10,600

Income tax rates 1988–9
Basic rate (first £19,300)	25%
Higher rate (above £19,300)	40%

Here are some examples of tax payments due, taking personal allowances into account:

- Single woman
  - annual income   £8,000   income tax   £1,349
  - annual income   £12,000   income tax   £2,349
  - annual income   £20,000   income tax   £4,349

- Married couple, husband sole earner
  - annual income   £8,000   income tax   £976
  - annual income   £12,000   income tax   £1,976
  - annual income   £25,000   income tax   £5,467

- Elderly single person, age 65–79
  - annual income   £5,000   income tax   £455
  - annual income   £8,000   income tax   £1,205

- Elderly married couple, ages 65–79; only husband has earned income
  - annual income   £6,000   income tax   241
  - annual income   £10,000   income tax   £1,241

INCOME TAX RETURNS

Your employer (if you have one) will tell the tax office that you work for them. You will receive an income tax form from the Inland Revenue which you must fill in and return within thirty days (hence the name 'return'). If your only income is from a job and you are taxed under PAYE by your employer, you may only receive a form once in every three years. The tax office uses it to check that you are still employed, and whether circumstances have changed. The employer does the regular work of giving the inspector of taxes information and paying the collector of taxes (by deducting income tax from your pay before paying it to you). You only have to deal with changes and additional income or allowances.

Remember that it is an offence not to fill in and return your income tax return on time. The onus is on the taxpayer to disclose income; therefore if you have a new source of income which you have not notified to the inspector, you should ask for a tax return or explain the circumstances in a letter.

THE 1988 BUDGET AND WOMEN

The 1988 Budget was radical in all sorts of ways, not the least of which was that it initiated a long-awaited and welcome reform to make the position of married couples more equitable in relation to tax. For many years husbands and wives have been taxed on their joint income unless they elect otherwise. Unmarried couples who live together have been taxed as separate individuals. In the 1988 Budget it was announced that some of the anomalies are to be removed – from 1990 women will be treated as tax-paying individuals in their own right. Women and men will be taxed separately, each in respect of all their income, whether from a job, savings and/or investments or capital gains, etc. From 1990, too, the Inland Revenue will write direct to wives, not to their husbands, and any tax rebates due to them will be sent direct to them. They will also be entitled to their own tax relief allowance on any capital gains tax they may pay.

Another change is that the recipient will not in future be liable to pay tax on any payments received under new maintenance agreements. The payer will receive tax relief (at the basic or higher rate) for payments up to a limit which is equal to the difference between the single and married person's allowance (£1,490 for 1988–9). Payments will be made gross.

Where a person is paying maintenance to more than one divorced or separated spouse, all payments will count towards the £1,490 limit.

Maintenance payments made to children will not qualify for relief, and they will not be liable to tax. School fees paid direct to a child's school will similarly not qualify.

TAXES ON CAPITAL
The current situation (since the 1988 Budget) is set out below.

Inheritance tax
This tax is payable on estates above a specified limit, but if the estate is inherited by a wife or husband no tax is due. It is also payable on any non-exempt gifts made in the seven years before a person's death. If you give away a specific sum of money (no matter how large) and live for more than seven years afterwards, then no tax is payable. However, if you die during the seven-year period some tax is payable on a reducing scale, depending on how long you live during that period.

There is an annual total exemption of £3,000 relating to gifts you may make. On marriage/dowry gifts this is to the total value of £5,000 from a parent, £2,500 from a grandparent and £1,000 from others. There is a small gifts exemption for gifts of up to £250 a person per year.

Capital gains tax
Capital gains tax is due if you make a profit on selling an asset, e.g., stocks and shares. The annual exemption is £5,000 for an individual and £2,500 for trusts for 1988–9. If you make a loss this year you won't get anything back on the tax you may have paid last year but the loss will carry forward to exempt some future gain.

FILLING IN YOUR TAX RETURN
The tax return form is now much shorter, simpler and more straightforward than it used to be; it even won a plain English award recently! You will find it much easier to fill in than previous versions. Before you face it, keep it in mind that many millions of people in this country pay income tax every year. It is thought that hundreds of thousands of them pay too much tax, either because they make mistakes or do not check on what they were

asked to pay! Make sure you don't come into that category.

The first thing to do is to make sure you fill in your tax return properly and the second is to check with your tax inspector that the assessment is correct and that your tax code itself is accurate. The tax code is given by the inspector to your employers. They use it to calculate how much tax they have to forward to the collector from your pay.

Take a look now at the tax return – there is an illustration of one below.

Inland Revenue Income Tax			
Tax return	Income and Capital Gains for year ended 5 April 1988 Allowances for year ending 5 April 1989		
H.M. Inspector of Taxes	Date of Issue	Reference	National Insurance no.

Please use the space below if you need to correct your name and address or wish to add any details. Is your postcode correct?

You may avoid delay if you use the reference and National Insurance number shown above when you write to or visit your tax office

Postcode _____

- You are required to complete this form, sign the declaration on the last page and send it back to me within 30 days.
- Before you start to fill in this form, please read "How to fill in your tax return." Look at each section before you write in your entries.
- If you are a woman and the return is addressed to you, make all your entries in the "Self" boxes and columns.
- If you are a married man and your wife is living with you, you must show all her income and chargeable gains.
- Remember to include all your income, even if you have already paid tax on it.
- Please be brief and give only the details asked for in the notes. If you do need extra space for any section, enter the total on the form and attach a separate piece of paper with the details.
- If you need help or more information, please ask me.

P1(1988)

Earnings

If you had earnings during the year ended 5 April 1988 from any of the sources listed below, please tick the appropriate boxes, enter the amounts for the year and give details in the space provided.

	Self	Wife	Self £	Wife £	Details including name and address of employer and job
Earnings from full-time employment	☐	☐			
All other earnings (for example, part-time or casual earnings)	☐	☐			
Profits from a trade or profession	☐	☐			
Tips	☐	☐			
Value of benefits in kind from your work	☐	☐			
Redundancy, compensation or other leaving payment	☐	☐			

Please tick if you received any of the other benefits listed below.

	Self	Wife	Details
Transport vouchers, other vouchers or credit cards	☐	☐	
Taxed sum from trustees of an approved profit-sharing scheme	☐	☐	
Unemployment or Supplementary Benefit	☐	☐	

	Self	Wife
If any part of your work during the year ended 5 April 1988 took place outside the United Kingdom, please tick here.	☐	☐

Pensions

If you received any of the pensions listed below during the year ended 5 April 1988, please tick the appropriate boxes, enter the amounts for the year and give details in the space provided.

	Self	Wife	Self £	Wife £	Details
Retirement or Old Person's pension	☐	☐			
Widow's or other state benefits	☐	☐			
Pension from former employment	☐	☐			

If you are receiving a pension now or expect to start one after 5 April 1988 but before 6 April 1989, please give the following information.

	Type of pension you receive now	Weekly £	4-weekly £	Monthly £	Quarterly £		Type of pension you are expecting	Date pension starts
Self						Self		
Wife						Wife		

If part or all of your wife's pension is paid as a result of her own contributions, please tick this box and give full details to claim wife's earned income allowance.	☐	If either of you were born before 6 April 1929, give your dates of birth. Self ☐ Wife ☐

Investments, savings, etc

If you received income during the year ended 5 April 1988 from any of the sources listed below, please tick the appropriate boxes, enter the amounts for the year and give details in the space provided.

	Self	Wife	Self £	Wife £	Details
National Savings Bank interest Ordinary account	☐	☐			
Investment account and Deposit bonds	☐	☐			
Interest from any other UK banks and UK building societies	☐	☐			
Interest from UK banks not already taxed	☐	☐			
Interest not already taxed from any other UK source	☐	☐			
Maintenance, alimony or aliment received (gross amount)	☐	☐			
Company dividends and unit trusts	☐	☐			
Other dividends, interest, etc, including income from trusts	☐	☐			
Rents from land or property in the UK	☐	☐			
Income from abroad	☐	☐			
Payments from settlements and estates (gross amount)	☐	☐			
Any other income or gains	☐	☐			

Remember to read the notes 'How to fill in your tax return' as you complete each section.

Outgoings

If you wish to claim for a tax deduction or any allowable payment which you made in the year ended 5 April 1988, please tick the appropriate boxes, enter the amounts paid in the year and give details in the space provided.

	Self	Wife	Self £	Wife £	Details
Expenses paid in connection with your work	☐	☐			
Subscriptions to professional bodies	☐	☐			
Interest on loans for buying or improving your home	☐	☐			
Interest payments on UK property for letting Number of weeks let ☐	☐	☐			
Other loan interest paid	☐	☐			
Covenants	☐	☐			
Maintenance, alimony or aliment paid	☐	☐			
Rents and yearly interest paid to persons abroad	☐	☐			

Capital gains

If you or your wife disposed of any chargeable assets during the year ended 5 April 1988:

Tick if:	If you ticked any of these boxes, please give:	
total combined proceeds exceeded £13,200 ☐		
chargeable gains (before allowable losses) exceeded £6,600 ☐	Description of asset	
you or your wife made an allowable loss ☐	Date of disposal	Amount of gain or loss £

Allowances

If you are entitled to claim any of the following allowances for the year ending 5 April 1989, tick the appropriate boxes and fill in the details asked for:

		Wife's first names	If married since 5 April 1987, date of marriage
Married man's allowance	Allowance for a married man living with or wholly maintaining his wife ☐		
	Self Wife	Local authority or equivalent body with which registered	Date of registration
Blind person's allowance	☐ ☐		
Son or daughter whose services you depend on	☐	Details see Notes for details required	
Housekeeper allowance	☐		
Additional personal allowance	☐		
Dependent relative allowance	☐	Name and address of dependent relative	

Dependant's annual income, excluding voluntary contributions	£	Relationship to you or your wife	Date of birth of dependant
If the dependant is not living with you please enter the weekly amount you contribute	£	What is the dependent relative's illness or disability?	
If any other relative contributes, please enter the weekly amount	£		

Death and superannuation benefits	Name of friendly society, union or scheme		
If you and your wife between you paid more than £85 in deferred annuity premiums in the year ended 5 April 1988 including any compulsory payments to provide annuities for widows and orphans, enter the total amount paid £	Full contribution for year ending 5 April 1989 £	Portion for life assurance relief and superannuation benefits (friendly society or trade union only) £	

Declaration Remember that you can be prosecuted for making false statements.

To the best of my knowledge and belief, the particulars I have given on this form are correct and complete	Signature	Date
Please give your National Insurance number in the box below, if not already shown on the front of this form. ☐☐☐☐☐☐	If there is any other information which you think may affect your tax liability, please give details here or on a separate piece of paper	

Printed in the UK for HMSO by Colibri Press Ltd. Dd. 8877025 12/87

As you will see, the form is quite short. If your affairs are complex you will get a different version of the form, and if you are self-employed or a partner in a business you will get yet another. Make sure you complete the correct form.

The tax return has two columns, for 'self' and 'wife' (it will take time to change things as a result of the 1988 Budget). If you are single, widowed, divorced or separated, fill in the 'self' box. If you are married, your husband should fill in both columns. Be clear about whether you are filling in the form in the capacity of a wife or of one of an unmarried couple. Also keep in mind the important changes which will be taking place in 1990.

First, deal with your earnings, how much you were paid in pay, overtime, etc. You can refer to the figure on the P60 form you get from your employer at the end of every tax year. Put a tick in the appropriate box and fill in the figure.

You also have to declare any other money you received – from any freelance earnings, tips, etc. In addition, you have to give information about any perks you get. These could be in the form of a season ticket or even a company credit card. Company car rules have become more strict in recent years.

You will see that you have to fill in details of any pension you receive. If you will become a pensioner in the next tax year you should include this information in the space provided. Sometimes a new pensioner may find herself paying too little tax at first and having to pay an ill-affordable extra sum later. Try to guard against this situation.

Any income from savings or investments will have to be included, but you don't need to give details of any investments which are tax-free, such as National Savings Certificates. You will have to declare any dividends you get from shares, unit trusts and the like.

Now we come to the outgoings, which is where you claim any allowances due. It may be worth checking the details with your local tax office; you don't want to find you are missing out.

Fill in the interest you pay on the mortgage, even if you pay the instalments net. Remember that if your mortgage is over £30,000 (which is the limit above which you do not get tax relief on the interest) and you and/or your partner pay higher rate income tax, you may need to obtain an interest certificate to send to your tax office. These are not usually required for mortgages as details are normally given to the Inland Revenue by the lender. For other loans an interest certificate will be needed.

Then, note that if you made capital gains on items like selling shares over the current exemption limit you should declare this in the capital gains box.

For the final section, allowances, look ahead to the next tax year and fill in any additional allowances you are or will be entitled to. You will also need to declare payments made under deeds of covenant.

Finally, add your national insurance number, sign the tax return, post it and relax. Your ordeal is over until next time!

THE TAX CODE

The following illustration is of a notice of coding.

Inland Revenue
PAYE

/

Please use this reference if you write or call.
It will help to avoid delay.

District date stamp

Notice of coding year to 5 April 198

This notice cancels any previous notice of coding for the year shown above. It shows the allowances which make up your code. Your employer or paying officer will use this code to deduct or refund the right amount of tax under PAYE during the year shown above.

Please check this notice. If you think it is wrong please return it to me and give your reasons. If we cannot agree you have the right of appeal.

Please let me know at once about any change in your personal circumstances which may alter your allowances and coding.

See Note	Allowances	£	See Note	Less Deductions	£
11	Expenses		25	State pension/benefits	
17	Age (estimated income £..............)		25	Occupational pension	
			25	Untaxed interest ...	
17	Personal		29	Tax unpaid £	
17	Wife's earned income				
				Less total deductions	
	Total allowances ...			Allowances set against pay etc. £	

Please keep this notice for future reference and let me know of any change in your address.
See Form P3(T) enclosed or previously sent.

Your code for the year to 5 April 198   is   see Part   overleaf

P2(T)(MAN)

This notice is what the Inland Revenue uses to tell your employer how much tax you should pay, and in which bracket you fall. Your employer then deducts the right amount from your salary cheque or wages. It is not at all difficult to understand.

First, there is a letter on it – this tells you, the tax office and your employer's accountant what your tax status is:

L means you are single, or a wage-earning wife
H means you are a married person or a single parent with a child at school
P means you are a single pensioner
V means you are a married pensioner
T means you don't want your employer to know if you're married or not (the tax office will keep your secret)
D in front of your code means you are probably taxed at a higher rate
F means you are taxed at a special rate to take account of your state retirement pension.

Then come the figures. They show how much you are entitled to in allowances. You can check this easily. Start with the basic tax-free allowance, add on any allowances due to you, and then subtract a figure for any tax you owe the Inland Revenue. Divide the whole by 10 (dropping the last digit). The result should be the same as the figure on the notice of coding.

If the two figures are the same, you'll be paying the right amount of tax. If they are not, get in touch with your tax office.

To be quite sure you are not paying too much tax, fill in your tax form and check your tax code to your own satisfaction. You may save yourself money, and even if you don't, at least you'll be satisfied that your tax is being handled correctly.

SAVING TAX

Here are some helpful tips:

- Be sure you have claimed all your allowances.
- Be sure you have included all your allowable outgoings and expenses.
- Check your tax code.
- Check that you haven't missed out on tax allowances in previous years (you can recover these for up to six years).
- Check that you are not paying tax on any redundancy money you have received or on any payment made to you in lieu of notice or because of personal injury. You shouldn't have to pay tax if your employer arranges things properly, unless you have had a redundancy payment of over £30,000.
- Check that you agree with your tax assessment – if you don't, contact your tax office.

- If you are working, see if you can save money and tax by asking your employer to provide tax-efficient fringe benefits (luncheon vouchers and/or petrol for your car, for example).
- Save tax by taking out a personal pension plan to supplement the one you have at work or in place of it. If you are self-employed, be sure to take advantage of possibilities available to you.
- Save tax if you can on income from any freelance or spare-time work. If you are self-employed – even in part – you may be entitled to claim for certain expenses at home that are relevant to your work. Examples are some costs of the room in your home which you use as an office, the costs of business travel and part of your telephone bill.
- If you are letting a room in your home, remember that you can claim some expenses. Include these on your tax return when you enter the rent you are receiving in the income column.
- If you have children and they are given money, remember they have their own tax-free allowances and watch where you can save money on their behalf.
- Retiring this year? Tell the tax office now in order to avoid overpaying or underpaying tax and having to claim it back or pay extra later.
- If you plan to make a gift of money to a charity, check if you could covenant it.
- Seek help when you need it from your local tax office, or from relevant organizations listed in the appendices.

SUMMARY
- Knowing where you stand in relation to income tax could save you money.
- Keep an eye on your position with regard to Budget changes. How they affect you may not be immediately apparent. Ask your tax office for information.
- If in doubt, ask – the Inland Revenue has helpful information and advice services. Their literature, too, is much easier to understand than it used to be.
- Don't be one of the many people in the country who pay too much tax.

Section 7

Concerning you as a woman

INTRODUCTION

As a woman you are not in the same position as a man; you have particular concerns and certain costs in life could hit you harder than a man.

These concerns are dealt with in this section.

COPING WITH THE COSTS OF CHILDREN

Children are a joy and a blessing – and they can be many other things as well. They are always very expensive. Today the total cost of bringing up a child (when everything is taken into consideration) can be not far short of £100,000!

The costs are high, even if you are part of a traditional family unit. If you are a single woman, the expense is, to say the least, daunting. Make sure you get all the financial help that you are entitled to.

Having a baby

All women get free prescriptions and dental treatment when they are expecting a baby, and for the following year. After the birth they can claim Child Benefit. There is extra help available for those on low incomes and for those who are single parents.

Before your baby is born

If you have to give up work to have your baby, you should get statutory Maternity Pay through your employers. Also, you could have the right to six months' maternity leave from your job. Both will depend on your length of service with your employer.

Maternity allowance

To be eligible for a maternity allowance you should have paid the required number of national insurance contributions (twenty-six out of the fifty-two weeks ending in the fifteenth week before the expected birth date). You can claim if you are employed or self-employed, but not if you have been paying reduced contributions as a married woman. Current rates are given in Appendix 6. Maternity allowance is not taxable.

Other payments and allowances are also available – consult your local DHSS office for details of all of them.

Once the baby is born

Child Benefit, One-Parent Benefit and help if you are on a low income are some of the benefits available. See Section 8. Consult your local DHSS office for specific information.

Education

Educating your children is a very costly business. Even if your children are going to a state school, there are many items to be paid for, from uniforms to school meals and school trips. The costs of private school education, of course, can be substantial; and boarding school fees, at some £3,000 per term, will make a sizeable hole in even a large income.

Planning the cost of your child's education costs, whether under the state scheme or a private scheme, is a matter of priority. There are many schemes to help you save for private school fees. It is important to be realistic about what you can afford. For information about the various plans available contact the Independent Schools Information Service; see Appendix 8.

Further and higher education

If you have a child aiming to go into further education (generally vocational) or higher education (generally for a degree), you can get help from your local education authority. The grant awarded will depend on your family circumstances and on the basic level applicable. This is fixed by the Department of Education and varies according to the type of accommodation in which the student lives and where they will be studying.

Check the position well beforehand. If your child does not apply, they won't receive a grant.

If you are a single parent, separated or divorced the grant will relate to your income if the child is living with you – even if you have remarried or are living with a partner who is not the child's father.

MARRIAGE AND LIVING TOGETHER

Marriage and/or living with a partner is one of the most daunting prospects faced by women, at the same time being one of the most exciting and potentially rewarding developments in terms of happiness and quality of life.

Both options involve issues that need detailed planning. There are many decisions to be taken, and there is a need to ensure that the relevant authorities are satisfied in relation to the legalities involved. Some of the decisions are financial ones.

Getting married

If you are planning to marry, remember that marriage will revoke any previous will that you may have made. You will need to review any other formal contracts you may have made to ensure that they are in line with your new situation in life.

As a married woman your tax position will be different. There are changes in the pipeline – see Section 6. In the interim, check that your personal allowance is used to reduce the tax you pay on your earnings (if any) or on any profits from being self-employed, and that you receive an allowance on your pension contributions. You cannot use these allowances to reduce tax on any investment income you may have.

Remember that when you are married you will have a normal single person's allowance in that tax year. Many people arrange to get married just before the end of the tax year; if you want to do that, plan ahead. There may be a queue for weddings at your local church or register office at that time.

If you elect for separate taxation on your earnings you will lose out on the swings (instead of getting the married man's allowance and the wife's earned income allowance, you will each get the single person's allowance) but you will gain on the roundabouts (the amount of taxable income allowed will be doubled before you start paying out in higher rate tax).

Separate assessment is a different matter – it won't affect your tax bill but it will mean that you will be responsible for filling in your own return and paying your own tax.

Social security benefits

The position is largely the same for women as for men. Some benefits (for example, Unemployment Benefit and state retirement pensions) will depend on your payments of national insurance contributions. See Section 8.

Second marriage

If you are marrying again following a divorce or being widowed, you will need to take care and spend time in reviewing your position. Much will depend on your individual circumstances. The basic point to remember is that, as on marrying for the first time, your new situation will mean that all contractual relationships will need to be revised. For example, you will need to make a new will.

If you are unmarried but living with a male partner

The position is largely the same as if you were married. You will, however, be responsible for your own tax affairs. If you have a child under 16 (or older than 16 and in full-time education or training) living with you, you can claim additional personal allowances.

Remember that you can't transfer any unused tax-free part of your partner's allowance to you to make full use of the allowances you both have.

The position with regard to social security benefits is largely the same as for married women, although you could lose if you were claiming some benefits. You can only claim for your partner if he is looking after your child and also financially dependent on you.

RELATIONSHIPS – SPLITTING UP

Your position as a wife or partner in relation to tax, benefits from the state, etc., is dealt with in other sections. Here we look at what happens if a relationship ends. At this time there may be many problems, not all of them financial. Financial matters can be very worrying and at a time of emotional upheaval anything that can be done to keep things under control is invaluable.

Getting help

If you are involved in a relationship which is breaking up and have little money, you will need help, urgently. What can you do?

Here are some tips which should be useful.

- First, inform those who need to know – such as your bank, building society or other lender – if you have a mortgage.
- Tell the bank quickly if you have a joint account. Either close the joint account and set up separate accounts for each of you or agree that both must sign for any withdrawal of money. Remember that unless you do that either partner can draw all the money out and also run up an overdraft.
- If you live in a rented house you will normally have the right to take over the tenancy if you are married and have been abandoned. Do be sure you continue to pay the rent! If you are not married you have the right to stay on only if your name is on the tenancy agreement. Bear this in mind when you become a tenant to avoid becoming homeless if things go wrong with a relationship.
- Talk to your local council as soon as you think you may have a housing problem. They will consider whether they can rehouse you.
- Talk, too, to your local DHSS office and Citizen's Advice Bureau to check on the benefits and help you can get. Ask whether you can apply for legal aid if there are likely to be matters needing a solicitor's services.

Relationships with your children
If you are splitting up with your husband or partner, you will undoubtedly be most concerned with the possible effects on any children you may have. You will be trying to keep things as normal as possible, difficult though this may be. Financial matters need to be put on a sound footing, but ideally they should not be discussed in front of the children.

Remember that you can get financial help from the state in certain circumstances, so do go and talk to your local tax and DHSS offices and ask for their helpful leaflets. See also Section 8.

Children and maintenance
Maintenance is the money paid by your husband or ex-husband to you or your children during a period of separation or following a divorce. It is in the form of either voluntary payments or enforceable payments made under a court order.

When a marriage or partnership breaks up it is likely that the

partner looking after the children most of the time will get
maintenance from the other. If the court order is worded so that
this maintenance is paid to the child it will count as the
child's income. Payments under court orders made before the
1988 Budget can be put against the child's personal allowance (the
same as the single person's tax-free allowance). If the court order
is worded so that the maintenance is paid for the children it
becomes the income of the person who receives the money.

LOST YOUR JOB OR INCOME?
If you have lost your job, lose no time in claiming Unemployment
Benefit. To get this you must be available for work and you will
have to sign a declaration to this effect. You will need to demons-
trate that you have paid sufficient national insurance contributions
(Class 1 contributions, paid by you as an employee) to qualify.
Check your position with your DHSS office if necessary.

You could qualify for an Enterprise Allowance if you have been
without work for at least eight weeks and are receiving Unemployment Benefit or Income Support when you apply. See Section
13 for details.

Other problems
If you are off work through ill-health, or are disabled or per-
manently ill, you can claim for help from the state. See Section 8,
and consult your local DHSS office.

BEREAVEMENT
Women are particularly vulnerable financially on the death of a
husband or a partner. This adds to the difficulty of coping at a
particularly distressing time. At some time in your life it is likely
that you will have to face this situation, or the death of a relative
or close friend. What do you do?

What to do if someone dies
It is important to build satisfactory relations with the executors of
the dead person's estate. They will be responsible for all detailed
arrangements, but there will be much for you to do as well. You
may yourself be an executor, of course.

For practical help, turn to any or all of your family doctor,

solicitor, bank, local minister of religion, DHSS office, local
funeral director and Citizen's Advice Bureau – plus your (or
their) accountant, if any. All of these can provide useful practical
advice and help. For example, the bank may be able to arrange a
loan to cover essential expenditure.

For support and comfort there are many groups outside your
family who will be ready to help. These range from Age Concern
to the Samaritans and include the specialist organizations for the
widowed and bereaved. You will be glad of all the support and
practical help available – it can often come from unexpected
directions.

The financial picture

Funerals can be expensive. If you are responsible for arrangements, check where the money for the funeral will come from.
The cost can usually be met from the money and possessions left
by the dead person, and under special circumstances help is
available from the state. Discuss your position with your local
DHSS office if necessary.

When it comes to dealing with the possessions and property of
the dead person, a lot will depend on whether there is a will. It is
a good idea to get advice initially from a solicitor about dealing
with the will and with probate or, if there is no will, about
handling the matter under the intestacy rules, whoever eventually
does the work.

If there are immediate money problems following the death,
which is frequently the case, it is important to approach the whole
matter logically and in the right order. Return the dead person's
order books, cheque-books, credit cards, passport, driving licence
and other such documents to the offices that issued them, and
keep copies of your letters. You should also tell the DHSS, the
Inland Revenue, and any employer, trade union or other relevant
organization, including bank and/or building societies and insurance companies. Try, too, to deal with insurance as soon as
possible. Check on car insurance in particular; if the car was
owned by the dead person, the insurance will die with the owner
and you may want to drive the car. Insurance policies and trade
union benefit papers will need to be sent to the insurance companies and trade unions concerned; they will then deal with any
payments and benefits due.

It is possible to deal with a will and with probate yourself (the legal authorization of what is done to put into practice the provisions of a will). It is, however, usually both simpler and quicker to have a solicitor to do the specialist work, if there is sufficient money to pay for those services. Some wills contain a clause appointing a bank to be the executor, with provision for their services to be paid first out of the estate.

Widows can claim special social security benefits and tax allowances; see Appendix 6.

If you have at least one child under 19 you can claim widowed mother's allowance. If you have no children and are 45 or over when your husband dies you can claim a widow's pension.

There are special allowances relating to tax after the death of your husband. Your local tax office will supply details.

Other help for widows can include help with the cost of the funeral, as already mentioned. Do ask whether you are eligible for benefit and, if so, what the extent of it is.

PLANNING FOR THE FUTURE – MAKING A WILL

Dying tidily is a service you can perform for those you will be leaving behind you. It will help them enormously in their time of grief if they know what your wishes were. Many problems can arise for them if you do not make a will.

Laws governing intestacy (dying without making a will) are still complex today, especially when applied to the estates of people involved in partnerships outside marriage. The surviving partner is often left to cope alone and can be at risk because a so-called common law husband or wife does not have the same legal status as a legally recognized husband or wife. If you are part of a partnership outside marriage it is particularly important to make a will to avoid trouble for relatives and friends, and to be sure that your wishes can be fulfilled.

Avoiding problems with wills

You need to do some careful planning of the provisions in your will if you want to avoid some very common problems. Here is an outline of the situation. If you live in Scotland or Northern Ireland, you will need to check up on the position: many details of law and practice are different there.

Home-made wills can cause problems if the simple but strict rules have not all been observed. It is perfectly possible to draw up your own will, but you need to know quite a lot about how to do it to be sure you handle the matter effectively. If you have more than a little money you should use a professional to ensure that your wishes are made clear, and that the correct procedure is followed. Here are some particularly important points to keep in mind:

- You must be careful about where you put your signature, and also about where the two witnesses of your signature sign (they don't have to read the will). It is wise to have witnesses who are fairly close to you, who are not relatives and who are younger than you.
- You must not ask anyone who benefits under the terms of the will to be a witness.
- You will need one or, more usually, two executors, or one plus a bank or solicitor, to secure probate and administer the bequests.
- You must be sure to date the will, to remember where you put it – and to let your family know where it is. Every five to ten years or so, check that the will is where you thought it was – firms of solicitors can go out of business or be taken over. However, generally they are very satisfactory safe-keepers of documents, as are banks.
- You should destroy any previous wills, or at least make it clear that the new will supersedes any earlier ones.

You can buy a will form from a stationer if you want to go ahead on your own. Do seriously consider having a solicitor to handle the whole matter, though; you can ask several to give you quotes – the fees charged vary widely. You can also discuss making a will with the specialist department of your bank.

No will?
Many women ask the question, 'Do I really need to make a will?' The answer is that it is probably much more important than you think.

If you don't make a will everything you own will be handled according to the rules of intestacy. Currently, this means that if you have children or other direct descendants living when you die, your husband will get only the first £75,000 outright, which may not even cover the value of your home, if it was in your name. Everything else you leave will be divided in two, 50 per cent going to the children (being held in trust for them if they are under 18) and 50 per cent going in trust to your husband. If any of your children have died before you and have no children of their own, their share will be divided up by those still alive; if they had children then their shares of your estate would have become part of their estates and will be allocated to their children (your grandchildren) on your death.

If you have no descendants living, your husband will get the first £125,000 plus half the amount remaining over this figure. The rest will go to your parents if they are alive, or to your brothers and sisters or their direct descendants if your parents are not alive.

'What happens if I am living with someone and not married?' is a frequently asked question.

If you are not married, on your death your partner may have grounds for making a claim on your estate. This can prove difficult and he could be awarded much less than if you had been married. That is why it is particularly important to make a will if you are in this situation.

Another reason for making a will is that you can make provision in it regarding who should be the guardian of any children below 18. This is obviously important if you are a lone parent, but it also covers those rare occasions when husband and wife die by accident at the same time.

Changing a will
You can make simple amendments to your will any time you want, by making a codicil. This is a document which has to be signed by you and dated and witnessed in the same way as the will itself. You can use different witnesses from those who witnessed the will. It is usually wise to get a solicitor to deal with a codicil.

Contesting a will
Women sometimes have to cope with the situation where an elderly relative such as a father or mother becomes dependent on a nurse or a housekeeper. There is a resultant worry that a will may be changed so that everything is left to the person concerned. Is there anything that can be done if this does happen?

The answer is that there is not very much. You might find that you had grounds for applying to the courts to rule the will invalid after the relative died, arguing that he or she was under undue influence or of unsound mind, but this is time consuming and can be difficult and costly. It is better to try to prevent the situation happening than to have to go to law afterwards.

Marriage

Marriage automatically revokes the will of either partner, unless the will has been drawn up in anticipation of the marriage. Remember that a single woman's will will have been based on very different considerations from those of a married woman; if you had a will before marriage it will need to be completely revised on marriage anyway.

Children

Be aware that the provisions for young children will be different from what is suitable for them when they are grown up. There are grandchildren to consider as well. It may take much time and discussion to decide on the most appropriate terms in a wife's and a husband's will to cover children and grandchildren, and also charities and other favourite causes, relatives and friends. Tax implications need to be borne in mind throughout. It is worth making the effort to avoid leaving problems for others.

Divorce and separation

These pose many financial problems for women. For example, a will may leave everything to a man's wife. If there is a divorce and the man plans to remarry, what is the position of the first wife?

Unlike marriage, a divorce does not revoke an existing will. However, clauses in a will made before divorce and naming husband or wife as a beneficiary may not remain valid. Divorcees should make new wills as matters could be complicated otherwise.

Separation does not affect a will. Even if there has been no contact between the couple for some years, a husband would still be entitled to inherit if he were a beneficiary in his wife's will, and vice versa. In a judicial separation, specific financial arrangements will have been made, and they may alter the situation.

Being cut out of a husband's will

It is rare for a wife not to be included in her husband's will, but it can happen. In that event the wife could have a claim on the estate under the Inheritance Act 1975. She would probably need legal advice to check whether it would be worth trying to establish it. The position is similar when a wife cuts a husband out of her will.

Inheriting a husband's debts

Another source of worry for the woman with a spendthrift or irresponsible husband is whether she is liable for his debts if he dies. And is she responsible for making any gifts of money mentioned in the will he has made if the estate does not cover them?

Briefly, everything the husband owned as an individual will be used to pay the debts as far as possible. This could include his interest in the home, if he and his wife were tenants in common. (See below for an explanation of the terms of tenancy.) Anything owned jointly by the husband and wife, such as a home (as joint tenants), car and bank account, all become the property of the wife and can't be touched to pay off the husband's creditors.

As far as gifts in the husband's will are concerned, or any possessions named in the will, these can only be passed on when all expenses for the funeral, legal and other costs and any debts, taxes, etc. have been paid. If every asset has been liquidated and there is not enough to pay off all the husband's debts, the wife won't be liable for any that remain – provided it is clear that the debts were the husband's own and did not involve the wife.

Keeping the home when the husband or partner dies

This is another key area for women. There are two options in house ownership: owning the home as joint tenants or owning it as tenants in common.

Under joint tenancy the wife or partner has no say in who will get her share of the home when she dies. It will automatically go to the other partner, the surviving joint tenant. Under tenancy in common, she can choose who gets her share; and so, of course, can the husband or partner. Tenancy in common is the option usually chosen by couples who have decided to live together or who are clubbing together to buy a home. Tenancy in common is particularly wise when the home is valuable. Each partner can leave their share to, say, a child. Then when the second partner dies the tax payable should be less because that estate will be smaller than the original joint one. Caution is needed before opting for tenancy in common as the degree of trust involved between parent and child is great; a parent could eventually lose out if a child did not keep to the original agreement. If the house is particularly valuable, both a solicitor and an accountant should be consulted before deciding which of the two options to select and also how to handle a bequest of a share in the house effectively.

SUMMARY

- It is important to recognize the particular financial problems faced by women, as distinct from men.
- Information, advice and help are easily and readily available.
- If disaster comes, life will be easier and less worrying if you have made basic provisions beforehand.
- Recognize the need to have a will, and the wisdom of consulting professionals to help in drawing it up.
- Be clear and specific in your will. This will greatly help your family at a time of difficulty and grief.

Section 8

A simple guide to state benefits

INTRODUCTION

*Every year many millions of £s of state benefits go unclaimed –
make sure that some of this money isn't yours!*

Those who miss out on state benefits usually do not realize
what they are losing, or do not know what to do about it. Here is
a quick and simple guide through the benefit maze.

The three types of benefit
1. *Contributory*. These depend on the national insurance contributions you have previously paid, and when you paid them.
2. *Means-tested*. These are available if your income is insufficient
   for you to live on.
3. *Special situations*. These give help in particular circumstances,
   for example, if you have a child you can qualify for Maternity
   and/or Child Benefit.

NEW DEVELOPMENTS
As from April 1988, the system has changed. Means-tested
benefits are the ones which are most affected.

Income Support has replaced Supplementary Benefit, and
interest-free loans have replaced one-off grants for items such as
furniture, clothes and perhaps even house repairs. Each DHSS
office has a fixed amount allocated to them, and they decide who
should receive a loan, according to priorities. If a loan has been
refused you cannot reapply for a period of six months. The
office's fund cannot be increased within the period it covers: once
the money is spent there will be no more until the next payment
period. Any loan will, of course, have to be repaid.

Also since April 1988, Family Credit has replaced Family
Income Supplement and Housing Benefit is calculated differently.

CONTRIBUTORY BENEFITS

If you are out of work, having a baby, ill, retired or widowed you may be entitled to benefit. But qualifying for the benefit, whether it is for you or someone dependent on you, will depend on whether you have paid sufficient national insurance contributions. If you have paid enough contributions, the level of what you will receive is standard, and it is not affected by what your husband or partner may earn.

There are four types of national insurance contributions:

- Class 1 – employed. Paid by employees between the age of 16 and retirement earning over £41 per week. Their employers also pay a contribution.
- Class 2 – self-employed. These are paid by self-employed people, defined as those paying Schedule D income tax.
- Class 3 – voluntary. You don't have to pay these, but if you earn only a small wage and don't pay Class 1 contributions, they could qualify you for retirement pension or Widows' Benefit.
- Class 4. This is not really a national insurance contribution at all, but a tax on the self-employed. It does not entitle you to anything.

See Appendix 6 for the current levels of benefits.

For more information, look at leaflets N140 (employees), N141 (self-employed), N127A (people with small earnings who are self-employed), NP18 (Class 4 contributions), N142 (voluntary contributions) and N1208 (contribution rates). These are available from your local DHSS office; some can be obtained at post offices, advice agencies and libraries. Alternatively, write to the Leaflet Unit, PO Box 21, Stanmore, Middlesex HA7 1AY.

MEANS-TESTED BENEFITS

If you are on a low income, or if you are unemployed or on your own looking after children, you could qualify for benefit. You could find, if you have a husband or partner, that the benefit is paid to him as the head of the household, so check up on this point if that would matter to you. Remember that the benefit will be based on the income of the whole family. You will get weekly cash help, the amount depending on what you have in savings and how much money you have coming in.

You can claim Income Support for help with day-to-day costs if you are out of work, working part-time, ill, elderly or caring for children or a disabled person. You can't claim if you have £6,000 or more saved (the sum you get will probably be reduced if you have more than £3,000 saved) or if you or your husband or partner work for twenty-four hours a week or more. There are many other caveats in relation to claiming Income Support. If you want to claim and are unemployed, ask for form SB1 when you sign on. If you are not signing on, for example if you are bringing up children on your own or are sick, you can get an Income Support Claim form from your local DHSS office.

Family Credit

If you have children and are on a low income, you could qualify for Family Credit – but only if you are working at least twenty-four hours a week. There are also other criteria to be met. You can find out how to claim from DHSS leaflets FC1 and N1261.

Housing Benefit

You can qualify for help with up to 100 per cent of rent and 80 per cent of rates in certain circumstances (but not if you are paying them to a close relative you may be living with, also not if you have more than £8,000 saved). This situation will, of course, change when domestic rates are discontinued, a process due to begin in 1990.

For further information, get DHSS leaflet RR1, *Housing Benefit – Help with Rent and Rates*.

The Social Fund

You can get grants or loans to deal with exceptional expenses you have to meet. These take in contributions to funeral costs (which have to be repaid by the estate), maternity and community care grants (to help with specific problems like lack of money following a marriage breakdown). There are also special Social Fund loans to help you budget and cope with facing an emergency. The loans will only be granted if you make an agreed weekly repayment and if you have demonstrated that you have or will have the ability to repay. You will also need to explain why there is no other help available to you from sources such as your family, charities, etc. The details of how to qualify and what to do are available in the following leaflets: FB29, *Help When Someone Dies*; FB8, *Babies and Benefits*; SF300, *Community Care Grants and Budgeting Loans*.

SPECIAL SITUATION BENEFITS

If you are bringing up children, there are several benefits you can claim. You may find that you qualify for more than one of these benefits, which are set out below:

- *Child Benefit.* Available if you are responsible for a child under 16, or under 19 who is in full-time education up to A level or a similar standard.
- *One-Parent Benefit.* Available if you are a single parent and live alone or are getting certain other benefits.
- *Guardian's Allowance.* Available if you are looking after an orphan.

To find out more get the following DHSS leaflets: CH1, *Child Benefit*; CH7, *Child Benefit* (for children aged 16 or over); CH11, *One-Parent Benefit*; N114, *Guardian's Allowance*.

If you are disabled or ill you can also qualify for benefits. You are eligible if you can't walk, if you are someone who needs a lot of looking after because you are physically or mentally disabled, if you are looking after someone who is ill and/or disabled and getting Attendance Allowance or if you have been injured at work.

To find out the details get the following DHSS leaflets: HB4, *Help With Mobility*; N1205, *Attendance Allowance*; N1212, *Invalid Care Allowance*; N1253, *Ill and Unable to Work*; N16, *Sickness Benefit and Industrial Injuries Disablement Benefit*. See also leaflets N12, N13, N1207 and N1237.

IF YOU ARE OVER 80

If you are on a low income, not entitled to a contributory retirement pension or your contributory retirement pension is less than the amount of the non-contributory pension and you have lived in the UK for the required number of years, you may qualify for a special retirement pension. Get DHSS leaflet N1184, *Over 80 Pension*.

CHRISTMAS BONUS

This is paid to pensioners, widows and certain categories of disabled people. You should get it automatically in early December. If you do, you could find out that you are entitled to some benefits you did not know about. See DHSS leaflet N1229, *Christmas Bonus*.

NHS BENEFITS

There are also several National Health Service benefits which could be available to you. These include free prescriptions if you are 60 or over; free prescriptions, dental treatment and vouchers for glasses if you are under 16 or on Income Support or Family Credit; free prescriptions, vouchers for glasses and free dental treatment if you are under 19 and in full-time education; and free prescriptions and dental treatment if you are expecting a baby or have a child under a year old.

There are also other benefits available in special circumstances. Contact your local DHSS office for details.

HAVE YOU BEEN TURNED DOWN FOR BENEFIT?

You can expect to be told whether or not you can appeal. Find out why you have been refused the benefit. Most claims can be referred to an appeal tribunal, hopefully an independent one. Be sure to check on this point. Get help if you want to appeal against a decision.

For general help and information in relation to the area of benefits, you can ring Freeline Social Security, 0800 666555 (0800 616757 in Northern Ireland). You can also get help and advice from your local Citizen's Advice Bureau or Consumer Advice Centre. Age Concern is another organization which offers help (see Appendix 8 for address).

SUMMARY

- The position with regard to state benefits is complex because there are many, covering widely differing needs.
- The many and varied changes made over recent months make the matter seem even more confusing. Further changes may be in the pipeline.
- The local office of the DHSS is the best place to make enquiries about the position as it affects you. You will find they have the relevant information and are friendly and helpful. See the appendices for other sources of information and help.
- Before you call in on your local DHSS office, take the time and trouble to marshal the relevant information so that they can answer your queries quickly and easily. If possible, have the relevant information written (or, preferably, typed out) so that it is clear and legible.

CASE-STUDIES

The next few pages illustrate some problems many women have to face, like divorce, loss of job, etc. They show what benefits you would be entitled to if you should find yourself in a similar position.

Case-study 1

Sarah is the unmarried mother of a 2-year-old boy, Carl. She has no husband or partner, no close relations and very few friends. She has been out of work since she became pregnant, nearly three years ago. She needs work but can't find anything suitable because of Carl. What benefits is she entitled to?

Sarah would, of course, be entitled to Child Benefit for Carl. She can also claim One-Parent Benefit and, if necessary, Income Support and Housing Benefit.

Case-study 2

Kate and Mark have an unhappy marriage. Mark has found another partner and Kate and he have agreed to a divorce which will be amicable, so that their two children, Fiona (5) and Clare (3), are not too upset. Will Kate be able to get support for herself and the children from Mark, and at what levels? What other benefits can she claim?

If their divorce is amicable, Mark will be liable to pay Kate maintenance for both herself and their children while they are separated, and for the children when they are actually divorced, until they are 16 years of age. In addition, Kate would receive Child Benefit for both Fiona and Clare and, after she and Mark have been apart for three months, One-Parent Benefit. She may also be entitled to claim Income Support and Housing Benefit, depending upon her financial status. However, if she claims both Income Support and One-Parent Benefit, then the amount of the One-Parent Benefit would be deducted from the Income Support.

Case-study 3

Mary is 23 and married to John, who is 28. They both have good jobs, earning approximately £15,000 each. Now Mary is expecting a baby. This means that she won't be able to work and they will lose her income. She hasn't yet decided whether or not to go back to work. What benefits can she claim?

Mary would probably receive statutory Maternity Pay from her employer. If she is not entitled to statutory Maternity Pay, she may qualify for state Maternity Allowance. After the child is born, she will be entitled to Child Benefit.

Case-study 4
Susan and Terry have three children. Susan doesn't work, but Terry does and they just manage. However, Terry has had an accident and will be in hospital for months. What benefits can they claim?

Terry is entitled to statutory Sick Pay, which is paid for up to six months. If he is still ill after this period, he will be put on to Sickness Benefit. He may also receive employer's Sick Pay. If this does not give them enough income, they can claim Income Support and Housing Benefit. Susan should also be able to get help with fares to the hospital to visit Terry if they are entitled to Income Support. This help is available by way of a Community Care grant from the Social Fund.

Case-study 5
Jane and Peter have been married for twenty years and have no children. Peter works and earns a good salary. He has paid into the company's pension scheme for years and also has a high interest bank account and some money in unit trusts. At 40 he didn't think anything would happen to him but, unfortunately, it did. Peter died of a heart attack, leaving all his money tied up and it will be months before the will is settled. In the meantime Jane is in difficulties, unable to get any money – not even for day-to-day expenses. How can she sort this out and what benefits can she claim?

Let us assume that Jane is also 40. She should fill in form BW1 and submit this to her local DHSS office as soon as possible. They will then immediately send her a Widow's Payment. At her age she would be entitled to £1,000, which should help her out until she can get hold of the money which is tied up. In addition, if necessary Jane could apply for Income Support, but if she does that she must be signing on and available for work. She may also be entitled to Housing Benefit.

Case-study 6
Sheila is widowed and has worked all her life. At 60 she is looking forward to retiring, but apart from a very modest employer's pension and £1,000 in a building society, she has no resources. She lives in a rented council flat. What benefits can she claim?

Sheila would be entitled to a retirement pension and in addition she may claim Income Support and Housing Benefit. She may also be entitled to NHS benefits.

Case-study 7
Malcolm Smith has left his home, wife and children, without a word. Tracy, his wife, now has the worry of surviving. She doesn't work and has children of 2, 4 and 7. She hasn't heard from Malcolm and doesn't know whether he'll send any maintenance or not. She has £500 in the bank but nothing else. What benefits can she claim?

Tracy would, of course, already be receiving Child Benefit. In addition she could claim Income Support, Housing Benefit and, after a three-month separation, One-Parent Benefit. If she did claim One-Parent Benefit, however, it would reduce her Income Support £ for £.

Case-study 8
Betty is a young unmarried mother, with two tiny children aged 9 months and 2 years. She needs to move to be near her mother so that her mother can help her. Betty has no money. She needs to provide for moving expenses and to get new furniture, etc. What benefits can she claim?

Betty would be claiming Child Benefit for her two children. In addition she would be entitled to One-Parent Benefit and, if this is not enough, Income Support. If Betty is moving a considerable distance, she would be entitled to a Community Care grant to help with furniture moving, etc.; this is not repayable. If her move is only local (i.e. a couple of miles), then Betty could apply for a budget loan, which is repayable.

Section 9

Women's finances and the law

INTRODUCTION

In this period of social advance it is important to review some legal issues applicable only to the financial affairs of women.

This section reviews this very important area.

There are two main ways in which the law can be seen to affect the financial affairs of women as individuals, as opposed to women alongside their male partners. Encouraging changes are now being made.

The first problem from the past lies in the effects of laws which ostensibly apply to both sexes but which in practical terms affect only one sex. The second is the effect of laws which either in their title or their content specifically provide (or deny) rights to one sex (usually women) with no equivalent provision for the other (usually men).

In the money area there are aspects of English legislation which provide examples of both problems. The former is illustrated by the inherent sexual bias of many long-standing property rights and some fiscal legislation. The latter problem is well illustrated by the fact that some recent efforts have had to be made specifically to redress historical imbalances, most notably the Equal Pay Act and the Sex Discrimination Act. Bankruptcy is an area where inequalities of the second type have not yet been resolved.

This section briefly describes the effects of some of the legal anomalies. It also outlines special provisions now being made and explains how they affect a woman's overall financial position.

THE MARRIED WOMAN'S PROPERTY RIGHTS

The 1882 Act

The first version of this Act was originally passed in 1882. It was amended in 1964. As originally passed, its purpose was to make you, if you are a married woman, a separate legal person in

property matters. It aimed to allow disputes about property
between you and your husband to be settled by reference to
current property rights legislation.

However, the problem was that for transfers of money for
housekeeping purposes you, as a woman, were deemed to be no
more than your husband's spending agent. The consequence was
that any savings you made continued to belong to your husband.
This was the case even though the same was not true in the
reverse direction. Where transfer was made from you as a wife to
your husband, that money or goods became entirely his property.

Married women became able to own property in their own
name for the first time. However, it was unjust that the major
source of money for most wives (housekeeping money) was not
owned by them. This led to some celebrated cases; one was that
of a wife who had used what she thought was her own half of joint
family money to enter the football pools and had a substantial
win; she found that not even half the winnings were legally her
property!

The 1964 Act
In 1964 the law was amended so that any surplus from a transfer
made to you as a wife for housekeeping purposes, and any profit
made from this, became jointly the property of you and your
husband. It did not, however, become half the property of each
(as proposed a year earlier). The distinction is analagous to the
two ways of jointly owning a house – see details in the information about wills in Section 7. In transfers in the reverse direction,
it remained the case that any housekeeping money transferred
from you to your husband became wholly his property.

There are therefore a number of points to bear in mind about
the Married Woman's Property Acts:

1. Despite their name, the Acts only slightly improve the property rights of a married woman.
2. Despite the 1964 improvements, women still have an inferior
   position to their husbands in relation to property rights.
3. The effect of the Acts may in practice be superseded by other
   contractual arrangements that a husband or wife may choose to
   enter into in relation to their property.
4. The Acts may be less relevant than formerly since women's
   property rights on divorce or on their husband's death are

provided for elsewhere in specific legislation relating to these areas.

5. As more and more women become part of the working population and have income of their own, the Acts' adverse direct impact is inevitably reduced.

6. The Law Commission is currently examining several aspects of this legislation. Further changes are expected to be made. Transfer of money to spouses is one matter that may be dealt with.

For most women the important thing about the Married Woman's Property Acts is that although they continue in force, they are less significant than in the past because of the impact of other factors. They can still cause you problems. The most likely impact on you is if you separate or are divorced from your husband without resorting to court action. Very often, how well you fare financially in a divorce situation will depend on how effectively your solicitor represents you. If a woman brings a valuable asset, such as a house, to a marriage it is as well for her to seek legal advice before marriage to ensure that if there is a divorce later she doesn't lose out.

WOMEN AND TAX LEGISLATION

The same social attitudes which gave rise to the need for the Married Woman's Property Acts also lie at the heart of the current bias against married women in tax legislation.

While the bias takes various forms, the main assumption involved has again been that a woman is nothing more than a legal annexe of her husband as far as financial matters are concerned. This does give rise to anomalies and many of these will be removed by the changes which are to take place from 1990.

Earned income

A married woman's earnings are currently treated as an addition to her husband's earnings. This means that if, for example, his earnings have caused him to pay a higher rate of tax, tax will be paid on his wife's earnings at the higher rate, apart from that part covered by her personal allowance (which is equal to the single person's tax allowance). This has meant that a number of married women have been discouraged from working.

In recent years this has been somewhat improved. Where it has
been financially worthwhile, the wife has been able to elect to
have her earnings taxed separately. However, this has not been
entirely satisfactory because only those who have made a conscious effort to make use of this provision have been able to
benefit. Husbands, of course, have not had to suffer any similar
provisions.

Investment (unearned) income and capital gains
Even worse than the treatment of married women's income has
been the treatment of investment or unearned income and capital
gains. The married woman's tax allowance relates to earned
income only; it cannot be offset against investment income (income from share dividends, building society accounts, unit trusts,
etc.) or capital gains (capital profits on the sale of property,
antiques, shares, etc.). A married couple has enjoyed no greater
allowance than a single person. Again this seems to have origin-
ated from the presumption that women are not financially independent. However, its perpetuation has been financially expe-
dient for successive governments.

Mortgages
Because a married couple are regarded as one unit for tax
purposes, married couples have one entitlement to tax relief on
£30,000 of a mortgage. Unmarried couples have qualified for two
entitlements to the tax relief, but there is one entitlement only on
mortgages beginning on or after 1 August 1988. This removes the
unmarried couple's tax advantage over the married couple.

Reform
In the 1988 Budget, the Chancellor of the Exchequer, Nigel
Lawson, made the announcement that he would be bringing in
major tax reforms substantially to change the tax treatment of
married women. Under these tax reforms, from April 1990 a
married woman will:

1. Have a separate income tax allowance and be taxed separately
   from her husband.
2. Qualify for her own taxation on investment income and have
   her own capital gains tax allowance.

There is also to be a provision to limit the cost to the Exchequer of the changes. In addition to being taxed separately, married couples will receive an extra married couple's (equal to the difference between the married and single person's tax-free allowance), but this will be available to the husband only, unless he does not work.

WOMEN AND EMPLOYMENT LEGISLATION

A woman's right to have the same access to work as men and to work under the same terms of employment and at the same rates of pay as men is one of the most important provisions that can be made in giving women equal opportunities. The two pieces of legislation concerned are the Equal Pay Act 1970 and the Sex Discrimination Act 1975, the former being strengthened by the Equal Pay (Amendment) Regulations 1983 and the latter by the Sex Discrimination Act 1986. In spite of the legislation, more remains to be done. Equal pay, for example, currently relates to basic pay only, not to fringe benefits.

The two pieces of legislation are not exclusively laws for women: neither theoretically applies more to a woman than to a man, and men are just as able to make use of them as are women. However, the Sex Discrimination Act and the Equal Pay Act were introduced because there was a need to get rid of traditional discrimination against women in employment (and, in the case of the Sex Discrimination Act, in some other spheres of life as well).

They are separate but complementary pieces of legislation. Both laws make provision for the elimination of direct and indirect discrimination in certain circumstances.

Direct discrimination

In both pieces of legislation direct discrimination is understood to be an action which can be judged to have been taken purely as a result of an individual's sex or marital status.

An example of direct discrimination covered by the Sex Discrimination Act would be an obvious and clear decision by an employer not to employ you as a woman for a certain job purely because you are a woman (or purely because you have children), provided that the employer was prepared to employ any man (or any woman without children) for that job. An example in relation to the Equal Pay Act would be some very obvious act of unequal treatment, such as paying a man a higher rate for a job than a woman colleague in the same job and at the same grade, even though both had equal abilities, length of service, experience, etc.

Indirect discrimination

This covers a wide range of situations, from only slightly disguised forms of direct discrimination to much more subtle mechanisms which it is all too easy to overlook. For example, a claim might be made that a woman should be paid less, or not be given a job, on the grounds of some spurious and unnecessary requirement which only a man could comply with, even though this was not necessary for the job (e.g. being able to carry a 40kg weight from a basement up several flights of stairs, when the need to do this did not ever arise in practice in that particular job).

At a more subtle level, a woman might appear to have absolutely equal pay and opportunities in every level within an organization and still be discriminated against. The organization could still effectively bar her employment at a particular level. One way of doing this would be to make attendance on a certain training course a prerequisite of promotion to the level and then to ensure that only male members of staff were selected for the course. On an equally subtle level an employer may, in advertisements, specify an age range such as 25–34 for a job; he knows that many members of the female workforce will be unavailable for work between those ages because they are taking career breaks to bring up children.

The Sex Discrimination Act and the Equal Pay Act are technically separate pieces of legislation, but they inevitably interrelate. Employing women in the same or similar jobs as men but restricting them to the lower paid jobs is sex discrimination on economic grounds, just as not employing women at all is.

It will be obvious that there is a considerable variety of ways in which women may be able to claim discrimination in pay and job selection. Some employers have devised quite bizarre routes to get round the law and industrial tribunals have generally upheld the rights of women involved in these situations.

New provisions of the Equal Pay Act

One new provision of the 1983 Equal Pay Regulations may not be immediately obvious and it is worth describing. This is the provision for equal pay for work of equal value. This means that even when one job in a firm is only done by you, a woman, e.g. clerical or secretarial work, while another is only done by a man (e.g. heavy lifting work) it is still possible for you to claim that the abilities and academic qualifications required are roughly similar and that you should, therefore, receive equal pay. This is an important breakthrough; under it a number of clever attempts at discrimination may be successfully challenged.

Taking action

Both Acts provide a similar grievance procedure; ultimately the matter can be brought before an industrial tribunal. This is a relatively informal court composed of a legally qualified chairman and two non-legal members who are experts in the particular area of industry and commerce concerned. While it may be possible to have an arbitrator from the Advisory, Conciliation and Arbitration Service (ACAS) appointed instead of going to court, it is possible that the case may eventually go to an industrial tribunal.

As industrial tribunals have significant powers to award compensation, to demand a change in job conditions and/or demand reinstatement, an individual can in practice have substantial rights. However, it is never easy for an employee to bring a case in spite of the theoretical protection given from victimization. It will perhaps take a considerable time and a large number of test cases for truly equal employment rights for women and men to become the norm. However, even so, the protection is now substantial and women are also protected in one or two other specific areas, such as the automatic right to have maternity leave while their jobs are kept open for them.

In short, as far as women and employment law are concerned, the position has certainly improved over the last twenty years. While there is some way to go, there is every reason to believe that changes will take place in employers' general attitudes, particularly as more and more employers become women.

SUMMARY
- Today the law is improving in relation to the protection of women's rights.
- It is important that women use those rights they have to the full and lobby against areas of injustice. In particular, further revision of the Married Woman's Property Acts is needed.

- Women should ensure that they remain as aware as possible of their legal rights, particularly in financial matters.

There are a number of other ways in which the law can be said to affect women and their financial rights, the most obvious of these being various provisions of the DHSS benefit system and some aspects of pension legislation. These points are covered elsewhere in this book.

Section 10

You and the money machine

INTRODUCTION

Every one of us – young, old, rich, poor, man and woman – has to handle or have something to do with money every single day of our lives whether we like it or not.

All too often, our knowledge is very basic and superficial and it tends to be focused on the area of spending money rather than on handling and saving it.

Often we have no concept at all of the money machine, the background of technology and administration which is behind simple transactions such as buying goods at the supermarket, using a credit card, writing a cheque or getting money from a cash machine.

We do not need to know the finest details. It is important, though, to understand how the money machine works – so that we can make it work effectively for us as individuals.

This section will focus on how the money machine relates to you. It will identify the services available, and show you how to make the best use of them. Finally, the section will spell out in detail some procedures for complaining and, more important, for getting things put right if services or goods prove unsatisfactory. Knowing how to ensure a successful resolution following a complaint is important; it could save you both time and money.

YOUR DAY-TO-DAY FINANCES

You use some parts of the money machine all the time to cope with your day-to-day finance. Your needs may be simple – to have money to buy what you want, and to have somewhere to put that money when you are not using it – yet a colossal industry exists to satisfy them. One reason is that we are living in an increasingly cashless society. You therefore need the services of at least one financial institution – such as a bank, building society or post office – to handle all the transactions involved in meeting your requirements.

Where do you turn for services from the money machine, what actual services are there on offer, and what is the cost?

BANKS

Banks still are the most popular and effective institution for dealing with your money needs. When you consider the mammoth scale of the operation they undertake you will, hopefully, have some sympathy with them when things go wrong, as they inevitably do from time to time. In recent years they have been reforming themselves to get rid of their old fuddy duddy image. Today you, the customer, are queen!

A major clearing bank in this country will be dealing with some 4 million personal accounts alone, and in addition handling huge amounts of work in relation to business and commercial banking both in this country and internationally. Every day there are transactions running into many billions of £s which have to be undertaken quickly and effectively.

We shall now look at the services on offer.

Current accounts

A current account will probably be your first choice – it enables you to do all of the following:

- Pay money into and out of your account, by depositing cash or cheques or having payments made direct to your account from some other bank or branch. Your employer, for example, can pay your wages or salary directly into your account; this is much safer for you than handling cash or even cheques.
- Pay bank drafts. The bank draws its own cheque payable to the person you want, deducting the value from your account. The draft is almost the same as cash and is particularly useful for deposits on houses or motor cars.
- Keep your money safe until you need to spend it or decide where and how you want to save it.
- Withdraw cash – either over the counter or by the use of an automated teller machine (ATM), now a familiar sight in or near banks and at other venues.
- Make payments to others on your behalf, direct from your account.

- Borrow, if the bank agrees.

Useful services resulting from having a bank current account include the use of a cheque-book and a cheque card guaranteeing that the bank will honour your cheque (to a limit of £50 at present).

The bank also offers standing order and direct debit services for current account holders. It is important for you to recognize the difference between these:

- *Standing order*. This is an instruction to the bank. It asks them to pay a certain fixed amount, usually each month or year, to some person or organization you identify (on a specific date if you wish).
- *Direct debit*. This is an authorization you give the bank to make payments from your account to a named organization. The payments may be fixed or you may give the recipient the authority to change these. The latter is called a variable direct debit. Variable direct debits may frighten the nervous because the control of your money passes from you to the organization to which you are paying the money. However, the arrangements have to be approved by the bank first, and the organization has to report to you what it is asking the bank to pay to them. There are rules to be observed and any payments made in error out of your account must be refunded.

Bank deposit and other accounts

There are many ways in which a bank will give you interest on money you don't need to use in the short term. Savings accounts pay interest and you can withdraw money from them at any time. Money market accounts pay more interest and you can still withdraw from these, though at pre-determined intervals, such as seven or fourteen days, or three months.

A word about bank charges

Banks do in effect charge for all their services. Bear this fact in mind: you may read about free banking and it may sound free, but it is not really free as you do not get any interest on the money you need to keep in your current account to avoid actual charges.

If you overdraw, you will be charged interest. It is likely that the interest will be at a higher level if you had no overdraft arrangement agreed in advance. Also, most banks will make transaction charges for a period of, say, three months if you are overdrawn, if only for a day. Charges can vary widely – from £7 to £17 or more for each period during which you have slipped into overdraft.

There is nothing wrong with a bank charging for its services, but it is important for you, the customer, to know about the charges and when they will be applied. They are usually based on the number of payments made into and out of your account. Free banking is usually available when you keep your account in credit. There are also high interest cheque accounts that are really a combination of a current and a deposit account.

Bank managers like to meet their customers, to explain what services they can provide, and to discuss any needs or problems with them.

THE POST OFFICE

The post office runs the National Girobank. This offers a similar service to that of banks, but there are differences. For example, a Girobank cheque can only be cashed at a post office (but there are some 20,000 post offices so it is reasonably easy to find one). The ATMs at post offices are linked with building societies rather than with banks. Charges for overdrafts are higher than those of the banks, but there is a levelling out factor: you are only charged for those days when you are overdrawn.

If you watch your money very carefully you could find that the National Girobank is cheaper than a conventional clearing bank. Note that if the National Girobank is privatized, there may be some changes in the system.

BUILDING SOCIETIES

Building societies are making a big pitch to handle your money on a day-to-day basis.

Savings accounts offered by them are used by about 28 million individuals. Some have a building society account to save a deposit for a home; others regard a society as a good place to make a secure investment and receive a steady income from the interest paid on savings. A growing number of people are using societies as banks and have cheque-books or cash cards linked to their accounts; others use them to accumulate savings for big items of expenditure, such as holidays.

Building societies' facilities vary widely, but it is usual for you to get at least some interest on your account. Services offered by building societies include:

- *Ordinary share.* Money can be paid into these accounts at any time during the working day (which includes Saturday mornings) and can be withdrawn without notice. Transactions are recorded in a passbook so that you always know how much is in your account. You can open an account with as little as £1.
- *High interest accounts.* In return for a larger minimum investment (normally £500 or £1,000) you can get a higher rate of interest than you get on an ordinary share account. You can withdraw without notice and with no loss of interest, providing you keep the balance of the account above a minimum level. Often the interest rate is progressively tiered according to the size of the investment so that larger sums of money attract better rates of return than the minimum investment.
- *Short notice accounts.* These offer you a higher rate of return than the ordinary share account, in exchange for which a period of notice of withdrawal (typically sixty or ninety days) is required. Immediate withdrawal with an interest penalty may be possible.
- *Term shares.* These offer you an additional rate of interest in exchange for your agreement to leave your investment untouched for an agreed period of time, frequently three or two years. The rate of interest on term shares is not guaranteed but the differential above the ordinary share rate usually is. Some term shares do not permit any withdrawals during the term except on death. Others allow premature withdrawals to be made in exchange for an interest rate penalty.
- *Regular savings.* Societies offer you preferential rates of interest to encourage regular monthly savings. These accounts are especially attractive if you intend saving for a deposit to buy your own home.
- *Save As You Earn.* Building societies also market Save As You Earn accounts as a special form of regular saving. These pay you a tax-free bonus if you contract to save a regular sum for at least five years. Their main appeal is to higher rate taxpayers.

New services from building societies – either alone or in conjunction with another financial institution – are being launched regularly. As a rule of thumb, decide what you need in terms of a service and then ask for it. The chances are that they will find some way of providing it.

NEW TRENDS

With the rapid pace of development in financial services, new products and services are being introduced constantly. What are these, and of how much interest are they to you?

Banks

The banks are increasingly packaging their services to identify your needs in relation to your age and your current and future lifestyle. At long last they have taken on board the fact that you need information and that providing this is an important and valuable part of the service they can offer you.

The particular services are aimed at your needs, as a student, a new home-owner, a young professional person or a parent; or as someone setting up in business, planning a happy, trouble-free retirement or needing help with saving and investment. Accounts are named to give a general indication of their nature: examples are saver plus accounts and home-owner reserve accounts.

Advances in technology mean that banks are able to introduce more services, some of which were impossible until recently. For example, in some banks you can now print out a copy of your own bank statement. Then there are the new-style 'smart' cards, which record information about your use of the card, showing the money you have spent, etc.

The chances are that if you go to the bank and tell them what you need they will have a service to meet that need. If not, you could easily have identified a new marketing opportunity, which in this marketing oriented age they will not be slow to develop.

COMPLAINING ABOUT GOODS AND SERVICES

The basic way to go about making a complaint is the same whether you are complaining about a faulty washing-machine or an unpaid insurance claim. The new financial services legislation does, however, help you to go further and, let us hope, faster than previously.

Once goods have been bought or services used (whether finan-cial services or any other kind), redress involves the money machine. See also Appendix 2.

Here we look at the general process you should go through if you want to complain; then we will look at the specific actions which you can now take in relation to financial services.

You should remember that there is no reason why you should put up with something you have bought if it is not satisfactory. Under the Sale of Goods Act 1979 and the Supply of Goods and Services Act 1982 you have certain rights. The Sale of Goods Act requires that the goods sold should be of merchantable quality – in other words, that they should be fit for their purpose – and also they should correspond to the description you were given. The Supply of Goods and Services Act requires that any goods supplied with a service must meet the same standards as those required by the Sale of Goods Act. Additionally the work done must be to a reasonable standard and at a reasonable price.

If you have bought something which doesn't work, you should try to get the matter put right as soon as possible. This is part of effective money management. Here is how to do it.

1. Be very sure that making a complaint is worthwhile. It will undoubtedly involve a lot of work and time and sometimes things can be unpleasant. If, however, you feel you have been wronged, then do something about it for the sake of others as well as yourself.

2. Think about what you believe is a desirable outcome for the complaint. Do you want simply an apology (frequently the most difficult thing to achieve, especially in the financial area)? Do you want the goods replaced or the services repeated, or do you want your money back?

3. Do your homework and know the strengths and weaknesses of your case, and your rights.

4. Keep it in mind that a reasonable tone of voice frequently works wonders. Try to keep the temperature down, even if you are hot under the collar!

5. Having decided you want to make a complaint, don't hang about; make your complaint as soon as possible. Old complaints are less likely to be settled quickly than recent ones. Remember, too, that you should first make your complaint to those who sold you the goods or services.

6. Be sure you make your complaint to the right person. Take the time and trouble to find out the person's name and, if

possible, arrange a personal visit to discuss the matter rather than writing or making a telephone call. Remember, too, that the element of surprise can be useful on occasions.

7. Put the case on record. Either through a follow-up letter or by leaving notes at the time of your visit, ensure that the organization you are complaining to has a record of what the complaint is about and also of the fact that you are making one. Put all the facts in writing: what you bought, what you paid, the nature of the complaint you are making and what you would like to see done as a result. If you can, enclose copies (not originals) of any relevant documents, bills, receipts, etc. Be sure that you can produce evidence of the fact that you have made all this material available – either ask for a signed receipt or arrange for material to be delivered in such a way that a receipt for delivery is available (via recorded delivery or registered delivery).

8. Follow up regularly, ensuring that you keep all records safe and that you keep a note of when you make a follow-up telephone call or send a follow-up letter.

9. If you feel you need help, get it. Look at the sources of help and advice listed in the appendices and decide which are relevant in your particular case.

10. As a last resort, if you are clearly in the right and can still get no redress it's worth writing to newspapers and magazines and to radio and television producers. They will sometimes cut through the red tape on your behalf.

11. If you do get satisfaction, or if you are dealt with sympathetically and quickly, do remember to say 'Thank you'. Dealing with complaints is generally a thankless task for those on the other side, and generally they are nothing at all to do with the original transaction which went wrong. Apart from showing that you are grateful for their efforts, you will be helping others who may later have to follow the same path.

COMPLAINING ABOUT FINANCIAL SERVICES

Complaining about financial services today and attempting to put right things that have gone wrong is an entirely new ball-game. It can be very confusing. This simple guide should help. The addresses of the institutions and organizations mentioned are included in the appendices. Many of them have useful literature available and there are special leaflets detailing the different Ombudsman services. In recent years the government has put through a great deal of valuable legislation protecting you as a consumer of financial and investment services. There are always risks in making money work, but once all the consumer safeguards are in place you should no longer easily fall prey to any negligence or sharp practice.

Insurance

It is important to remember that there are several laws concerned with insurance. These regulate and provide protection for policyholders in case an insurance company fails. There is also a variety of self-regulating procedures. How to seek redress, therefore, is complex.

You need first to determine the nature of your complaint and where you feel the failure lies. It could be with the company selling you a particular policy, or with an intermediary, someone who sold you a policy on behalf of an insurance company, such as an insurance broker. It is probably wise not to try to decide for yourself the technical description of what caused your problem. Leave such terms as 'negligence', 'misrepresentation' and 'unprofessional conduct' to the experts. Say clearly what your problem is, preferably avoiding terms such as 'swindle' and 'confidence trick' as those could leave you open to legal action if someone has simply made an honest mistake that can easily be put right.

It is also important to recognize whether there is an investment element involved – if so, that could involve another set of official rules as well.

Complaining against an insurance company

You should first contact the company itself. Write to the manager of the branch that issued you with the policy. If this fails, try the chief executive at the company's head office (the address will be on the policy). In both cases try to write to a named individual – perhaps the person who signed the policy or an authoritative letter or proposal.

If you do not get a satisfactory response, contact the Association of British Insurers (ABI), the trade association for most insurance companies. Check whether the insurance company belongs to the Insurance Ombudsman scheme. If so, you could

take your case up via the Insurance Ombudsman. There is also a
Unit Trust Ombudsman who is completely independent, but is
responsible to the Council of the Insurance Ombudsman Bureau,
which administers the service.

Complaining against an insurance intermediary, broker or agent

Take the matter up with the company or person involved. If the
broker is a member of the British Insurance & Intermediaries
Association (BIIBA) write to ask them to take up the complaint
with the broker and to let you know the result.

If that does not have a successful outcome, write to the Insurance Brokers Registration Council (IBRC). All brokers must be
registered by law and IBRC has a disciplinary committee that can
cancel a broker's registration if he is found guilty of unprofessional conduct. Ask them to investigate your complaint.

Building societies

The system for building societies is similar to that for insurance. If
you have a complaint against your building society, try to deal
with it first at your local branch office. If you have no satisfaction
from them, contact the chief executive at the society's head office.
If you still have no helpful response, write to the Building
Societies Association (BSA) with details of your complaint. The
probability is that your society will be a member of the BSA.

If you still have no result, you can take your case to the
Building Societies Ombudsman if you think that the society has
acted wrongly financially or morally (which might mean it is in
breach of its rules or of the Building Societies Act 1986) or that it
has given you unfair treatment, or that you have suffered unduly
through bad administration. You will need to establish that you
have suffered loss, expense or inconvenience. The Building
Societies Ombudsman scheme covers problems you may have
with regard to services or investments made through a building
society.

Banks

Follow a similar route if you need to make a complaint to your
bank. First try to sort it out with your branch manager. If you
don't get anywhere, send the details to the appropriate general
manager of the bank (generally classified as the general manager

of UK retail banking or something similar) at the bank's head office. Ask your local branch manager for the name and job title.

If this approach does not give satisfactory results, you can refer your complaint to the Banking Ombudsman, but find out first whether this approach is appropriate by checking the rules of the Banking Ombudsman's office to see if your problem falls within the terms of reference.

Investments

The provisions of the new Financial Services Act require all investment businesses to be authorized; it is a criminal offence to carry on investment business without authorization. The Act defines investment business; this includes dealing in investments, arranging deals, managing and advising and selling financial investment products such as life assurance and units in unit trusts. Note that its provisions apply only to investment businesses in this country.

Here again, the procedure for complaint is as for other sectors of financial services. You should complain first to the organization which handled your business. This must be authorized by the Securities and Investments Board (SIB), or one of the Self-Regulatory Organizations (SROs) or a Recognized Professional Body (RPB) such as the Institute of Chartered Accountants or the Law Society.

If you have suffered loss as a result of a breach of the rules of the SIB by a directly authorized business or through a breach of the SRO's or RPB's rules, you can take legal action for damages. Hopefully, this won't be necessary. You should be able to obtain satisfaction before this from the schemes set up by the organizations themselves.

With effect from late August 1988, you are covered by a compensation scheme if you lose money.

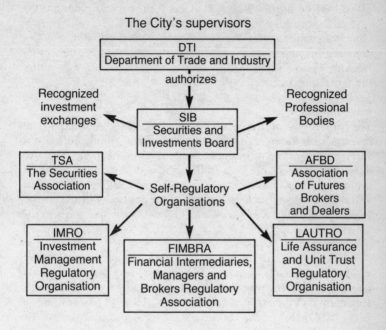

The City's supervisors

Complaining to the SROs

Under the new legislation, you now have recourse to the relevant
SRO. For example, the organisation concerned will be the Life
Assurance and Unit Trust Regulatory Organisation (LAUTRO) if
the complaint involves the marketing of a unit trust, and it will be
the Investment Management Regulatory Organisation (IMRO) if
the complaint relates to other forms of investment of your money.
If you are dealing with a financial intermediary and want to
complain, the chances are that you will need to contact the
Financial Intermediaries, Managers and Brokers Regulatory
Association (FIMBRA).

Your money-go-round

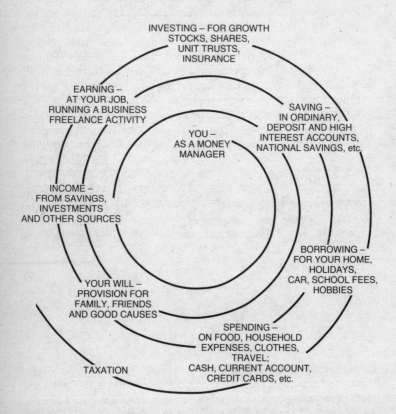

INVESTING – FOR GROWTH
STOCKS, SHARES,
UNIT TRUSTS,
INSURANCE

EARNING –
AT YOUR JOB,
RUNNING A BUSINESS
FREELANCE ACTIVITY

SAVING –
IN ORDINARY,
DEPOSIT AND HIGH
INTEREST ACCOUNTS,
NATIONAL SAVINGS, etc.

YOU –
AS A MONEY
MANAGER

INCOME –
FROM SAVINGS,
INVESTMENTS
AND OTHER SOURCES

BORROWING –
FOR YOUR HOME,
HOLIDAYS,
CAR, SCHOOL FEES,
HOBBIES

YOUR WILL –
PROVISION FOR
FAMILY, FRIENDS
AND GOOD CAUSES

SPENDING –
ON FOOD, HOUSEHOLD
EXPENSES, CLOTHES,
TRAVEL;
CASH, CURRENT ACCOUNT,
CREDIT CARDS, etc.

TAXATION

Money-Go-Round was the title of the author's London Weekend Television series.

SUMMARY

- If you take a little time and trouble to familiarize yourself with the way the money machine works, it will pay you dividends metaphorically as well as literally.
- Today most of the large organizations are constantly introducing useful new products and services. Banks, the post office, building societies and insurance companies, are tending to offer overlapping services. It is worth spending some time in considering carefully where to shop for financial services. Having decided, develop your relationship with that organization.
- Remember that it's your money. Don't be afraid to ask for the type of product or service you need. The chances are that it can be made available to you in one way or another.
- If you find you have a problem, don't hesitate to complain about it and attempt to seek redress. The way you set about this can have a direct effect on whether you get the solution which you are seeking to your problem. Find out how to make a complaint in the most effective manner – to get results rather than just making a fuss. It's time and trouble well spent.

Section 11

You and your home

INTRODUCTION

Your home is the centre for your family life. It is also likely to represent the biggest investment you (or anyone else in the family) will ever make.

There are many financial aspects to be borne in mind in relation to your home. This section tries to help you decide on the priorities for you. It covers the key issue of whether to rent or to buy your home. It sets out the pros and cons, and also includes some useful tips.

It also goes into the procedure for buying a home. Different kinds of mortgage are outlined to help you make your choice, and there are also notes on the tax position.

With regard to renting property, attention is drawn to some priorities and the landlord's responsibilities are identified as well as the tenant's. In addition there are notes on home improvements, including the finance and legal aspects.

PROPERTY AND WOMEN

Women increasingly find themselves in the position of having responsibility for running, renting or owning a home. This can happen to you in one of the following ways:

- You as part of a couple choose to share in the responsibility.
- You inherit the home in entirety on your husband's or partner's death.
- You are left with the home after your marriage has ended or a relationship has broken up.
- You look after it while your husband or partner is away for extended periods – perhaps working abroad – or, perhaps you look after it because that is the choice of you both.

- You are on your own and have decided that home ownership is a good investment for you or that you would be wise to rent your own home.

RENT OR BUY?
The first and most basic question you have to consider before going into property is whether you should rent or buy.

The pros and cons of renting
- Rent is often less than the interest and capital repayments involved when buying and owning outright, and it is usually easier for the property and the rent to be shared than it is when buying.
- It can be more convenient for short-term occupation.
- It may relieve you from some of the additional expenses and responsibilities of home ownership; e.g. the landlord may do some of the repairs and may deal with making and paying for some arrangements such as cleaning and heating.
- You have some protection in law from eviction or excessive rent provided that your tenancy is in a residential dwelling, you have exclusive possession of at least one room in the property (except in Scotland), the rateable value of your part of the property does not exceed £750 (£1,500 in London) and the rent you are paying is at least two-thirds of the March 1965 rateable value (this is the 1988 position; when domestic rates are discontinued the rules will be amended).
- You have nothing to show for your money. You pay your rent and even after many years you end up without owning anything.
- You may have to pay management fees and service charges.
- You lack full security of tenure.
- You lack full independence.

Finding a home to rent
Much will, of course, depend on your circumstances. If you have absolutely nowhere to stay, your local council could regard you as homeless. If you have children, are elderly or disabled or have a violent partner, and in certain other circumstances, you could qualify as a priority case and in law the council must then find a home for you.

If you cannot qualify for immediate council help, where do you look to find yourself somewhere to live? There are three basic options open to you:

- *Renting through a private landlord.* You need to talk to local estate agents and scan your local and national newspapers, relevant magazines, etc.
- *Renting through your local council.* You will need a lot of patience as it could take years for your name to get to the top of the housing list. The sooner you put it down, the better.
- *Renting through a housing association.* This is a relatively new and increasingly popular way of renting housing. Some housing associations are charities that provide homes for renting, often to the elderly. Some are business enterprises which, again, may be involved in letting to specific groups. Others are cooperatives which help people to buy their own homes; the people paying rent to those are at the same time making a stake in buying their own homes. Today housing associations are able to get good levels of support, both from local authorities and from the private sector. The government-created Housing Corporation is the supervisory body for them.

In addition to those options, you can get a licence to rent property; many landlords offer rented property under this arrangement. It can be a good working arrangement but you will need to check the details. Talk to your solicitor if you have one, or enquire at your local Citizen's Advice Bureau.

Landlord's responsibilities
The landlord has specific responsibilities which vary depending on whether they relate to weekly renting or renting over longer periods. For example, for weekly renting a rent book is required, but for longer renting it is not. In short lets (under seven years), the landlord is responsible for all structural and external repairs, plus repairs and maintenance to all sanitary and heating appliances. For leases or lettings of seven years or more, responsibility for repairs, including damage caused by natural ageing, etc. needs to be spelled out. If furnished accommodation is being let, the landlord must ensure that it is fit to live in when the tenancy commences.

Remember that a landlord can only be held responsible for repairs he has been told about.

Tenant's responsibilities
These should be stated in the tenancy agreement, which is then
signed by both parties. They can include internal decoration,
repairs and keeping the property in good repair. You could be
presented with a bill for 'dilapidations' on departure, so always
make an inventory and a note of the decorative condition when
you move in. If you fail to adhere to the terms and conditions of a
valid tenancy agreement you could be evicted.

Sharing rented accommodation
Ensure that each tenant's name is entered in the rent book or
agreement. Protection under the Rent Acts only applies to named
persons; if you are not named, you will have no protection should
the named person(s) leave the accommodation.

Insurance of rented property
The landlord is responsible for the fabric and structure of the
accommodation. As a tenant you should insure your own personal
belongings, and also the interior decorations as you will be
responsible for them. Make sure you find out precisely what the
position is.

The pros and cons of buying
- Historically, property has always been a good investment.

- You can buy property freehold or leasehold; if the latter, the
  longer the lease the better. (But you may find it difficult to get
  a mortgage for a freehold flat, except in Scotland.)

- You have full independence, which for many people is important.

- Home-ownership is regarded as a factor in your favour, e.g.
  when you are applying for credit or borrowing.

- After you've finished paying for your home, you have a substantial (and saleable) asset.

- Your money is tied up in bricks and mortar, sometimes causing
  liquidity problems.

- The responsibilities of home-ownership can be expensive – in
  terms of both time and money.

The key considerations

On balance, it is nearly always better to buy if you can afford it. Once you get a foot on the property ladder, you can later climb further up.

A flat is almost always sold leasehold (when your lease expires the flat belongs to the land-owner). A long lease (say, 999 years) presents no problem, but a short lease (say, under 55 years) could be extremely difficult to obtain a mortgage for or to sell, though the Leasehold Reform Act may help in this situation, giving the owner of the lease the right to buy the freehold. You usually have to pay an annual ground rent and, for a flat, possibly a service charge to maintain the overall property. The leaseholder must also comply with any rules and regulations relating to the use and management of the building.

Whether you can afford to buy a home is, of course, an important consideration. You need to ensure that you can cope with the repayment costs, and also that the property you are buying is worth at least as much as and ideally more than the price asked. Then if you find you have difficulty in keeping up with the repayments you can sell without being left with a debt.

The rule of thumb with regard to mortgage lending hasn't changed much over recent years. The bank, building society or other lender will normally lend some two and a half to three times your annual salary for a mortgage lasting 20–30 years, usually with a smaller proportion (up to approximately one and a half times the annual salary) for a second earning partner. These multiples are, however, only a guide; the ultimate determining factor in how much will be lent is the borrower's ability to repay. If you are thinking of borrowing more, there is no doubt that in these days of easy access to credit you will be able to do that, especially if you can show satisfactory records of income and expenditure. It is, of course, most important not to undertake too much in terms of financial commitment, no matter how attractive the prospect of owning your own home is. After all, you will want to enjoy living in it, and if you are constantly worried about money this won't be possible.

Some tips on renting

Renting
- Avoid informal arrangements and oral agreements. Get proper

advice and always have a written tenancy agreement drawn up by a solicitor or estate agent acting in your interest. This will give you some security, particularly under the Rent Acts. You need a rent book if the renting is done on a weekly basis.

- Make sure you really understand your rights and responsibilities under the lease or licence, in particular what it is your responsibility to pay for and what it is the landlord's responsibility to pay for.

Some tips on buying
While you are looking around
- Set up your mortgage arrangements in principle.

- Line up a solicitor or conveyancer to help with the legal work. Solicitors' charges are based on the work they have to do for you, so you may want to discuss this and agree a figure. It is not essential to use a solicitor; if you use another organization to draw up the conveyance, make sure that it carries out all the necessary procedures.

Once you have seen the property you like
- Make an offer 'subject to contract and satisfactory survey' – this gives you flexibility to negotiate on the price if the survey discloses adverse features, such as subsidence, dry-rot, wood-worm, etc.

- The relationship between the advertised asking price and the offer you make is dictated by market conditions in the area in which you are buying. When property is in demand, you can expect to have to offer at, or very near, the asking price to have any hope of obtaining the property.

- Keep a watchful eye on whether or not there is a danger of being gazumped (this happens when the vendor accepts a higher offer).

When your offer is accepted by the vendor (those selling)
- Tell your solicitor, who will need to know the name(s) of the vendor(s) and their solicitor as well as full details of the property you hope to buy. The estate agent should help to see that nothing is left uncovered. Your solicitor will then receive or prepare a draft contract for approval which will be discussed with you. You will also be asked to authorize the legal

searches at the Land Registry, local authority and council; these are made by your solicitor to check if anything adverse is recorded against the property, such as a public right of way across the garden or rights for adjoining property-owners.

- Organize your mortgage – more is said about this later in this section.
- Ask a chartered surveyor to do a survey of the property for you. This can either be a short survey which will list any obvious fault or, if you wish, a full structural survey which will cost you more but will tell you all that you need to know about the house you are buying. If the building society or bank which is giving you the mortgage does a survey (for which you will pay), this will be for its own purposes and you will probably not see it. You are strongly advised to have one done yourself. It is possible to arrange for a surveyor to do a valuation and a structural survey or house buyer's report at the same time, which saves money. This should be discussed with the lender at an early stage in the proceedings. Buying a house is the biggest transaction you are likely to undertake, so go into it with your eyes wide open.
- If the survey reveals adverse aspects, see if you can negotiate on the price, but don't risk losing the property by arguing over trivial points which can easily be put right.
- At the offer stage, you may be asked to pay a deposit. You are not legally bound to do so until contracts are exchanged – see later – but you may feel a small deposit is worth making as a gesture of good faith and genuine interest in buying the property. It does not give any security against gazumping.

When you are quite satisfied about the price you are paying, the condition of the property and the legal matters relating to it
- Sign the contract (which will be drawn up by the vendor's solicitor), but only after your solicitor has agreed it. Even at this stage you are not legally committed to the purchase. You will, however, cause a lot of inconvenience to other people in the chain (those linked with you in the sale/purchase of properties) and make yourself very unpopular if you pull out at this late stage.
- On a pre-arranged date your solicitor will literally exchange your signed contract for an identical one signed by the vendors of the property. At this point you will be asked formally to pay

a deposit, usually 10 per cent of the purchase price. You are now committed to the transaction and must go ahead with it. If you don't, the deposit will be forfeit.
- On exchange of contracts, you become liable as the purchaser of the property for the insurance on it, so you must get this organized as well – see Section 4. Legally you also become liable for any repairs to the new property, although if disaster happened before you actually moved in, such as a fence blowing down or a water-tank bursting, you would normally negotiate with the vendor over who pays. Be sure you know exactly where you stand so you don't have to pay while the vendor is still in possession.

Completing the purchase
- This is usually fixed for twenty-eight days, or thereabouts, after exchanging of contracts, to allow the solicitors time to prepare the legal documentation required to transfer the ownership of the property from the vendor to you.
- During this breathing space you will be very busy:
  - Arranging for a removal firm to take your belongings to your new home on or after the day the purchase is completed. (Check on the removal firm's insurance for handling and transporting your belongings, and if it is not adequate get your own insurance cover organized.)
  - Getting new carpets, curtains, etc. organized if necessary.
  - Making sure that the gas, electricity and telephone will all be connected and working on the day you move in, and also checking that meters have been officially read and billing has been organized.
  - Organizing your mortgage and finance so that you can pay for the property. The money usually changes hands via a banker's draft, which is a cheque that does not need the normal time for clearance. Your solicitors will need this – in effect, they exchange this with the vendor's solicitors for the keys.
  - Just before completion your solicitor will need your signature on the legal document required to transfer ownership of the property to you.
- It sometimes happens that the vendor does not meet the completion date, in which case you may need an accountant's advice as well as that of your solicitor, in relation to extra

expense and inconvenience to you. If you are late in meeting the completion date yourself (usually because of delay in settling your side of the finances), you become liable for interest at a rate specified in the contract.

- On completion your solicitor will provide you with a completion statement detailing the total cost to you. He will also send you his bill and expect it to be paid almost immediately, or it may form part of the completion statement itself.

If you are a first-time buyer you will only have the details outlined above to worry about.

If, however, you are selling a house as well as buying one, you will have a lot more to think about. You will have the procedure above to deal with both as vendor and as buyer, and you will have to make sure that the two transactions coincide – otherwise you will find yourself without anywhere to sleep or with two houses, both costing you money.

WHEN YOU NEED A MORTGAGE
Whether you are buying jointly with a partner or on your own, you should find that the situation regarding availability of mortgage facilities and the basis on which a loan will be granted is as set out earlier in this section. Do make some enquiries before making an offer to a vendor – most people get an agreement in principle from a financing institution before they start looking at properties.

Joint ownership
Co-owners, for example a wife and her husband (or partner), normally own their property as joint tenants. Technically, there is a 50:50 division of purchase price or sale proceeds. On the death of one of the parties, 100 per cent ownership goes automatically to the survivor who would then be responsible (this is why it is important to have mortgage protection insurance; see information below about mortgages). The alternative is to purchase as tenants in common. This divides the purchase price or sale proceeds between the parties, i.e. in accordance with the contributions. Each then owns that specific share and can leave it in their wills to persons other than their tenants in common. The survivor may not have a right to continue to live in the whole property.

The latter procedure is the road to explore if you are considering buying your new home with one or more friends. See the information in Section 14 about wills; a house is especially valuable. Do remember, though, that you could have problems if a co-owner sells their share; that could mean that in the future someone with whom you may not precisely see eye to eye will be a co-owner with you.

Different kinds of mortgage

Repayment
You pay interest and make repayments on capital at the same time, so the amount you owe is reduced year by year. To start with, your regular repayments will be nearly all interest. As time goes on the interest element lessens and the capital repayment element increases. This is known as a normal repayment mortgage.

A variation to help first-time buyers is the low-start scheme. This offers an increasing repayment mortgage, whereby the repayments increase as your tax relief on the interest element gets less.

You would expect to have this type of mortgage in conjunction with a mortgage protection insurance policy – a cheap and practical form of life assurance which covers the outstanding loan in the event of anything happening to you before the mortgage is fully paid off. If you have no dependants this cover is unnecessary.

Endowment
You pay interest only on the loan, and the capital element remains outstanding. It is repaid from the proceeds of the endowment policy at the end of the term of the loan. Endowment policies have two particular advantages: they include life assurance and they are easily transferable. If you want to convert your mortgage to a larger one to buy another house, you simply take out another endowment policy.

The low-cost endowment policy is the most common type. It pays off the loan at the end of the mortgage and usually provides an extra tax-free lump sum. It is important to remember that there is no guarantee that anything more than the original loan will be paid. There are low-start endowment policies; with these the payments are at lower rates for the first five years. They are particularly attractive if you can be sure that your income will rise during that time.

A full endowment involves a larger outlay. It should give a substantial tax-free lump sum at the end of the term. It is not a common choice of house buyers.

Finally, there are unit-linked endowment policies. The premiums are invested in unit trusts which are intended to pay off the mortgage when they mature. There should also be an additional tax-free sum on maturity; that depends on the performance of the investments. There is some risk and this type of policy is not a wise choice for the faint-hearted, but there is also the prospect of greater profits.

Pension mortgage

Instead of taking out an insurance policy to provide the funds for paying off the capital, you make payments into a pension plan. Then, when you retire you use part of the lump sum that the pension plan provides to pay off the mortgage. You will qualify for tax relief on the contributions both to the pension plan and on the mortgage interest. One disadvantage of this type of mortgage is that the pension plan cannot be used as security, so you will need a life assurance policy as well, which adds to the cost.

Remember, too, that the amount that can be commuted if you want a tax-free lump sum is limited. This, of course, also reduces your level of pension payments. Future tax and other changes could also adversely affect your pension payments.

Other types

These are many and varied. They include:

- *Shared ownership schemes*. Run by some housing associations and local authorities. They are particularly attractive for young first-time buyers as they help them to get on to the housing ladder. You own part of your home, and on the rest you pay rent. As and when you can afford it, you can buy more of the share in your home.
- *Government home loan schemes*. These are based on saving regularly. After two years, if you buy a cheap enough home, you can qualify for a cash bonus of up to £110 and a loan of £600 to be added to your mortgage loan.
- Further options include index-linked loans, long-life mortgages and guaranteed mortgages.

Lenders are increasing in number. While the banks and building societies still dominate the market, finance houses, credit companies and some investment houses are entering the market. New types of scheme aimed at making borrowing easier appear frequently – but nothing ever comes for nothing, so it is wise to compare alternative schemes before choosing.

The principles for you to follow remain constant:

- First, find out how much you can afford.
- Choose a house or flat which is basically right for your range of income and for your needs.
- Shop around for the right organization to lend you the money in the most suitable form. Time and effort spent on finding the right deal for you is probably one of the best investments you will ever make.

WHICH TYPE OF MORTGAGE?
A question almost everyone asks is, 'Which type of mortgage is best?' The answer is that it depends on what you want.

Of the three main types described above, the pension mortgage is the most expensive in terms of monthly outlay, but it does provide a very useful benefit for someone with no pension scheme.

Of the other two, the endowment mortgage is generally slightly more expensive than the repayment mortgage, but this is more than offset by the bonus you can expect at the end of the mortgage term if you go in for a with-profits policy.

On the other hand, many people go for a repayment mortgage because it is cheaper in terms of monthly payments, and also you can actually see your mortgage decreasing as the capital is repaid – albeit very slowly at first. There is also the possibility of extending the length of the mortgage; this can be useful if rates go up and you cannot meet the repayments.

The income tax position and mortgages
The 1988 Budget brought in a radical change. Until 1 August 1988 the £30,000 loan limit for tax relief on mortgage interest on your sole or main residence was linked to the borrower. It was thus possible for two or more unmarried people buying a property together to get tax relief individually on the interest on mortgages

of up to £30,000. For new loans the relief is now restricted to one amount of £30,000 per property, however many people are buying it together. Joint purchasers have the tax relief apportioned between them according to their individual borrowings.

MIRAS

Through MIRAS (Mortgage Interest Relief at Source), the interest you pay is reduced by the level of basic rate tax whether you pay tax or not. Effectively, on an interest rate of 10 per cent, you save nearly 2·5 per cent (you pay 7·5 per cent). Most people with mortgages get their tax relief this way. If, however, you are borrowing more than £30,000 and did so before April 1987 you may be an exception. If you do not know, ask your mortgage company whether you are in MIRAS and whether they can arrange this if you wish to exercise your option to have basic income tax deducted at source under the scheme. It does not apply to higher rate tax, nor does it extend the relief beyond the statutory limit of £30,000.

SHOULD YOU REPAY A MORTGAGE LOAN IF YOU CAN?

Another question often asked in relation to mortgages is whether you should repay your mortgage if you receive a lump sum which would make that possible. The answer, of course, depends on you – on your outlook, upbringing and general philosophy of life.

If you hate owing money, then go ahead and repay the mortgage. You will avoid paying more interest. But remember this will mean you lose the chance to invest elsewhere to supplement your income, and your money will be tied up in your house. You may be able to get more interest by investing the money than you would be paying in interest net of tax for the mortgage.

If you want to repay some of your mortgage, it may pay you to do it in December rather than January. This is because some lenders work out the next year's calculations on the amount owing at the end of the year. Find out the position in your case.

Remember too that it can cost you something extra if you ask the bank or building society to terminate your mortgage early. It means extra administration for them and they may charge you for this.

If you can meet the mortgage repayments comfortably and have learned to live with them, let them continue. You will get the tax relief on the interest, and you can keep any lump sum you may have for use in some other way. You never know when you might be glad of it.

In difficulties paying the mortgage?

We all hope that things will go well, but life sometimes doesn't work out that way. What do you do if you find you are having difficulties in making your regular mortgage payments?

You should alert the mortgage lender as soon as you see a problem on the horizon. Bear in mind that they have the legal right to take you to court to repossess your home if you fall badly into arrears. Luckily most major lenders are sympathetic with the problems which sometimes have to be faced and will try to help in practical terms. These can include arranging for the mortgage to be repaid over a longer term or, with a repayment mortgage, paying the interest only until the position has improved.

The next thing to do is consider whether you can increase your income by any means. This is not as impossible as it may sound. For help in considering the options talk to your local Citizen's Advice Bureau or Money Advice Centre.

THE ROLE OF INSURANCE

Remember that you should carefully consider your options with regard to insurance when you are buying a home. You need to insure against illness and unemployment, and to protect the mortgage. The cost of the cover is modest in comparison with the peace of mind it will buy you. See Section 4 for detailed information.

HOME IMPROVEMENTS

Once you have got your own home, you will want to make it as comfortable as possible and to improve it from time to time. Home improvements are always good value – they make the home better for you and can add to its resale value.

Remember, however, that since 6 April 1988 it has not been possible to get tax relief on the interest on loans taken out to extend or improve a home.

Before you improve your home there are three main considerations to bear in mind.

Finance

If you are modernizing your home, you could be eligible for a local authority grant, whether you are an owner or tenant (but grants of this kind to owners or tenants are discretionary and availability will differ throughout the country). You must also obtain permission from the owner of the property if you are a tenant. There are four types available:

1. For major improvements, such as providing a kitchen or bathroom.
2. For smaller improvements, such as the installation of hot and cold water, associated repairs and/or replacements.
3. Repair grants for substantial structural repairs on older properties.
4. Special grants for owners for putting in other standard amenities and means of escape (if necessary).

Applying for a grant and going through the procedure involved is complex. Do remember if you are following this path not to pay any money to your builder until you have notice of the grant in writing. It can be risky to have the work started before official authorization.

You can also apply to your bank or building society to extend your existing mortgage. They may ask for a survey before granting the money. Remember to check up on the current position in relation to whether your MIRAS and interest payments would be affected; this could result from changes in the 1988 budget.

Legal matters

You should ask your solicitor to check the deeds of your home to see if there are any restrictions on improvements. Also talk to your bank or building society before undertaking any work. In addition, you should inform your insurance company as your insurance premiums could be affected. (You are legally bound to tell them everything relevant to what they are insuring, at all times.)

Planning permission and related matters

Check up on your position. Building disputes are a very good source of revenue for lawyers! One piece of good practical advice is to ensure that you use a reputable builder, preferably a member of the Federation of Master Builders. Any firm you use to do improvements to your home or, indeed, to provide you with any service, will be bound by the Supply of Goods and Services Act. Despite this, there are many cowboys. The Office of Fair Trading (its address is given in Appendix 8) has some practical and useful literature on the subject. Do write and obtain it before you embark on home improvements. You will find your time – and your money – are used to better effect if you do.

SECURED LOANS

To repeat the warning given in Section 5, be careful about secured loans at apparently advantageous rates, especially if they are linked to the clearance of all your other debts. They may help you in your particular circumstances, but they may cause problems. You must make sure you do not take on one you cannot afford.

A secured loan is generally one secured as a second mortgage on your house. Therefore, if you fail to keep up the repayments you may find you lose your house.

REPAIRS

Repairs are often a source of worry to a woman living on her own, unless she has a friendly neighbour to call on or has taken a course in DIY! Where do you go for help?

In a real emergency you may have to call on one of the many twenty-four-hour services advertised in the *Yellow Pages* and in local papers. That may be expensive, and unless you act on someone else's recommendation you can't be sure of the quality of service you will get.

If you have time to shop around before getting large jobs done, get estimates from firms recommended by family or friends, or firms which you know are well established in your area and which are members of a professional institute or trade association. Then at least you should be able to get some protection if things go wrong.

HOUSING OPTIONS FOR OLDER WOMEN

If you are an older woman, you will have particular needs.

Maybe you and your husband no longer need as large a home and garden as you had when the family were all living with you.

Maybe you are on your own now and you don't want to have to

cope with all the work and responsibility of actually owning and running your own home.

Maybe, because of increasing age or some disability, you need a particular kind of accommodation or regular supervision.

There are a number of schemes to suit these differing needs and the organizations mentioned in Appendix 8 which have special concern for the elderly will be able to provide information and put you in touch with others which can help.

Some of the schemes available

- *Accommodation to rent*. Mainly from local authorities and housing associations. This includes sheltered accommodation with warden services. Sheltered housing usually has self-contained accommodation plus communal facilities such as a sitting-room and guest-rooms for relatives coming to stay.
- *Council housing*. If you wish to rent from the council, you need to get your name down early – waiting-lists are long. Sometimes council house exchanges are possible.
- *Accommodation to purchase*. In many parts of the country there are developments with the elderly in mind. It would be worth looking out for local advertisements placed by builders putting up retirement houses. It is possible to buy sheltered housing in some areas.
- *Residential accommodation*. This is sometimes offered by specific organizations helping people who can satisfy certain criteria or have special needs.

Help with repairs

Repairs are a big problem for elderly home owners, especially if money is tight and most of your savings are in your home. Some schemes which can help are:

- *Home income plans*. A mortgage loan is raised on the property with the help of an insurance company or building society and is used to buy an annuity to provide extra income for life. The loan is repaid on your death or on the sale of the property. The advantage is that the house remains yours. There is an age qualification involved; usually you must be at least 70.
- *Home reversion schemes*. Under a typical scheme, you sell your house to the company operating the plan. The actual sale does not take place until your death. Until then, there is simply a

change of property title. Your home is then leased back to you
for the rest of your life for a nominal rate, say £12 a year. You
will then get, either as a lump sum or in the form of an
annuity, between 50 per cent and 100 per cent of the value of
your home, the level being higher the older you are. Care is
needed when considering this option – remember that you
can't get your house back. Sometimes you can find you are still
responsible for repairs and other expenses. Also, you may not
get the full value of the house, which would reduce the amount
you could pass on to your family.

- *Financial help with repairs*. Consider house improvement grants
  from councils, and help from some financial institutions and
  building societies which have special loan schemes for the
  elderly.

RUNNING YOUR HOME

The costs of running a home are always higher than we imagine.
Here is a very brief checklist with some tips which should be
helpful.

Insurance

This is dealt with in Section 4. The areas of importance you
should cover are:

- Rebuilding costs, including architect's and surveyor's fees and
  temporary housing
- Possessions.

Remember that there are many factors which will be taken into
consideration in the premium quoted. These include:

- Where you live (inner cities have the highest premiums)
- Whether you have any valuable items
- Whether your house is unoccupied during the day
- Whether you have a history of making claims against insurance.

Rates/community charge

Rates are really a tax imposed to pay for local services, such as
roads, police, rubbish collection, education and the like.

The system works by assigning your home a rateable value.
Every year the local authority sets the rate for the year at a

specific figure in every £. The demand comes in March and there are options for payment: one lump, two sums (April and October) or instalments (usually ten in the year, monthly from May to February).

The rates system is to be superseded by the new community charge system, scheduled for introduction in 1990. This will be paid by all citizens and it is thought that local authorities will set this around £200–£250 a person per annum.

The new tax is being introduced to spread the cost of local authority services more evenly across the population. The previous rates system imposed large burdens on those owning property while others paid nothing at all towards the cost of the services they were using every day.

Clearly the new system will need time to settle down and procedures will need to be established to ensure that those with low incomes don't suffer hardship. If you are in this category discuss the matter with your local DHSS office.

PAYING THE BIG BILLS
The costs of running a home include regular bills which often seem to be larger than they should be and to arrive at the most awkward time!

These include bills for:

- Energy (gas, electricity, coal etc.)
- Water
- Telephone.

There are ways in which banks and building societies can help you to spread the payment of these so that they are less burdensome. You can also spread the electricity and telephone costs by buying stamps at your local post office, but these stamps do not earn interest and a better option is to save small sums regularly so you can pay the bills when they come.

SUMMARY
- Getting a new home, whether it is bought or rented, should start with reading up on the subject. Time spent on this will help you to avoid problems and save you money.
- Be as clear as you can about your objectives and about your own position. You will then be better able to brief and instruct

others so that they can do what you want efficiently, and also cost effectively.

- Housing is a complex matter which includes many different aspects that need to be considered. Nevertheless most people arrive at a satisfactory outcome.
- It is useful to keep a small notebook, setting out the different areas on different pages. In it you can keep a record of what is happening and have an at-a-glance guide to the progress you are making toward your specific requirements and objectives.
- As indicated at the beginning of this section, investment in your home is likely to be the biggest financial transaction you ever make. A little extra care, time and trouble could save you money and make the money you spend on your home go a lot further.

Section 12

Savings and investments

INTRODUCTION

*Most of us look forward – at some time – to having money which we
don't have to use immediately. We will want to ensure it is safe, and
hope that it will grow. To achieve that we need to save or invest.*

This section will outline how to determine your investment
strategy and decide what to do with a lump sum. It will signpost
the options which you should consider for regular and lump sum
savings and investment. Handling savings and investments and
knowing what to do with a lump sum payment can be a difficult
aspect of money management. It is important that it is done well.

This section concentrates on lump sum investment. That lump
sum may be a windfall or it may have been amassed over a period
through regular savings. There is a checklist which shows different
ways of investing and includes regular savings schemes.

The starting point

Capital investment is a regular experience for only a few of us;
expertise is built up over the years if we are in this category. For
most of us it happens once or twice in a lifetime, and we certainly
cannot afford to learn the hard way – by our mistakes.

A lump sum can come into your hands in a variety of ways:

- From a pension fund or a redundancy payment
- From the sale of your house
- From receiving a legacy
- Following divorce or widowhood
- From the maturing of an insurance policy
- From a win on the races or in the football pools, even!

However you got this money, you will want to consider carefully what to do with it. You face opportunities and decisions which
perhaps you have never faced before. You need knowledge you
never expected to need, and you may be bombarded with advertisements and leaflets offering it. How do you choose? Where do
you start?

KNOW YOURSELF

First, you need to assess yourself, your life and your needs. Do
you need money now? Are you likely to need it in five, seven or
ten years' time, and can you tuck it away meanwhile? How old
are you? Are you single and alone and likely to remain so? Are
you one of a couple or a member of a family with whom you wish
to share your money? How large or important is the lump sum – is
it large enough to make a big difference to your life, or just a
little? Are you earning? Are you paying tax? If so, at what level?
Have you time to concentrate on relatively complicated investments like shares, whose prices you need to watch frequently?
Would you rather be free from having to think about investments?
Above all, how do you feel about risk? Are you something of a
gambler who would want to have a little fun, aiming for capital
gains but recognizing risks – or is security all-important to you?

One basic question is whether you want to invest for income or
for growth.

Inflation

To be sure that your money is available for a rainy day, and is also
providing you with some extra income, it must be invested with as
much guarantee of security as possible. The safer the investment,
the lower its possible growth rate. You will want to be sure your
money can, as far as possible, retain its real value against inflation. Even with a modest inflation rate of 5 per cent a year for
five years, £1,000 will have to increase to £1,276 in five years if it
is to buy what your £1,000 does today. Most bank and building
society accounts have in fact given more than 5 per cent over the
last five years and inflation has been generally lower than that.

Can you consider being more adventurous than a bank or
building society with at least some of your money? Remember
that you can really only afford to take risks if you are sure that it
would not materially affect your lifestyle if the investment fell in
value.

Know your tax position

Your liability for income tax should influence your choice of
savings and investment plans. If you pay no income tax, take full
advantage of the schemes such as the national savings ones, in
which interest or dividends are paid gross, i.e. with no automatic
deduction of income tax. If you have only modest savings, pay no
income tax and your savings are with a building society or bank,
you could increase the interest paid to you by roughly a third
simply by moving your savings into a scheme in which interest is
paid in full, or gross.

For those in the opposite situation, your capital gains tax
annual allowance can be put to good use if you are a high rate
taxpayer and need more income for a time. It can help you draw
the tax-free equivalent of an income by cashing in slices of capital
investment year by year, if you need the money.

Boosting your pension fund

An important consideration, if you are in work and either in a
company or personal pension scheme (or eligible to be so), is the
possibility of boosting your pension fund. Special tax incentives
allowed if you put money by in your pension fund make this a
most effective investment option. Any capital available could be
added to your pension, either as an additional voluntary contribution to your regular pension scheme or as a separate single
premium payment. Because of the tax benefits, the government
limits the proportion of your earnings which you can put tax-free
into a pension fund. Too few of us use up the maximum allowed.

You should also take advice on whether a one-off contribution
now could be related to any previous years' earnings. See Section
14 for details.

Pay off, or reduce, your mortgage?

In paying off a mortgage loan over twenty-five years, you have to
pay back more than twice what you borrowed at current rates – a
sobering thought. Perhaps you would derive particular personal
satisfaction from either reducing this burden or repaying the
whole sum. Bear in mind that if you pay it all off you may exclude
yourself from getting home improvement or other loans from your
mortgagee. You should also weigh up against paying off the
mortgage the advantages of letting the tax-assisted mortgage

continue, leaving your newly acquired capital to work better for you elsewhere. Another factor is that paying a mortgage off early may involve cash penalties.

SPREAD THE RISK

Here are some suggestions of modest lump sum investments offering basic security. Later suggestions will be more adventurous; as your total available to save or invest rises, you become more able to spread the risks.

If you have a sum of, say, £2,000–£5,000, put some of it into a safe national savings scheme and – provided you are a taxpayer – put some in a bank deposit account, or money market account or building society for easy access.

If you have a sum of between £5,000 and £10,000 your options are greater. You can choose between a mix of national savings/bank/building society/government stocks/insurance-based savings products and special services. You can also consider equity investments, purchasing stocks and shares, such as blue chips, either directly or through appropriate unit trusts which allow you to spread your risk.

If you have a large sum to invest, say £40,000 or more, play safe with around three-quarters of it and have some fun with the other quarter. You could select some stocks and shares or other investments which hopefully will offer you greater reward, albeit for greater risk. Special investment services from banks and building societies could be helpful here, and so could the services of investment advisers.

A brief glance at some of the options

National savings

The Department for National Savings, established on 1 October 1969, has responsibility for all forms of national savings. These are schemes which provide absolute safety and offer something for everyone's needs. All post offices have explanatory leaflets. If you can lock your money up for a while, consider putting something into National Savings Certificates, Deposit Bonds, Yearly Plan or Premium Savings Bonds. Taxpayers will be liable to income tax and/or capital gains tax on interest from some national savings schemes; be sure to check up on this.

National Savings Certificates. These are a form of government security, redeemable at the purchase price plus a previously stated amount of interest. The interest is tax free and increases over five years; therefore for the best return they should not be redeemed until five years after purchase. Every issue is on sale until a new one, linked to current interest rates, replaces it. You receive the advertised rate of interest regardless of any changes in interest rates generally, which is good when rates fall after you've bought your Certificates, but not so good if they rise.

Index-Linked Savings Certificates. These are also worth considering. Here the return you receive is limited to the inflation rate plus whatever bonuses the government announces.

Deposit Bonds. These are sold in multiples of £50, with a minimum purchase of £100 and a maximum of £100,000. Your money will earn interest, credited yearly. The current rate is 9 per cent.

Yearly Plan. This scheme was introduced in July 1984 to replace the index-linked Save As You Earn scheme. Each plan lasts for five years, with a fixed rate of tax-free interest.

Premium Bonds. You will get no interest from these, but will have a chance of winning a prize of up to £100,000. The maximum holding for each individual is £10,000.

Gilts

Gilts are stocks issued by the government and its enterprises. They are called gilts because originally the certificates were edged with gold as a sign of their trustworthiness. There are several categories, classified according to the redemption dates and/or the way the interest is calculated.

A dated gilt bears a redemption date on which the full face value of the stock will be repaid to you. So, for example, you might invest £90, the market price, in a gilt of £100 face value. You will receive a specified rate of interest calculated as a percentage of the face value. At the date specified, you will be paid £100. Interest is usually paid twice yearly.

Like other stocks and shares, the price of gilts fluctuates from day to day, so take advice before venturing into this field. Gilts are useful for those who want a lump sum return at a given future date and can tie up their money until then. But, unless the issue is index-linked, interest will remain fixed throughout the lifetime of the gilt, which makes it unsuitable for someone who needs an income from them which keeps pace with inflation. However, many people buy gilts as they buy company shares, aiming to buy when they look likely to be profitable and to sell just before they begin to be unprofitable.

Gilts are issued by the Bank of England, and are bought and sold on the Stock Exchange through a stockbroker, bank or financial intermediary, or through the Department for National Savings – in which case you apply direct to them. Income tax is not deducted from interest payments on gilts bought through the National Savings Stock Register at a post office, which makes this the best route for non-taxpayers.

For further information on gilts refer to literature produced by the Public Information Department of the International Stock Exchange (address in Appendix 8) or ask for leaflets in your local post office.

Income from gilts is taxable and is usually paid after deduction of basic rate tax, which you can reclaim if you are not a taxpayer. (See above regarding gilts bought at a post office.) Capital gains on gilts are not taxable at the time of publication.

Banks, building societies and insurance companies

These all provide wide ranges of products and services. Their leaflets are plentiful and easy to follow, so shop around to find the schemes which best suit your needs.

Generally, the longer you can afford to lock your money up and the more you have, the higher the rate of interest it will earn. If you want your money back quickly you are not likely to get the best rates.

Having at least some of your money in a bank or building society will often give you access to other useful facilities, such as somewhere to keep your valuables or the use of a cash-machine card, and sometimes it will give you access to your savings via a cheque-book. The interest rates are competitive and with inflation at a low level a useful rate of return can be achieved. There is a wide spread of options with regard to terms of investment, access, interest rates and other factors.

Banks and building societies pay interest after deducting basic rate tax; non-taxpayers can't reclaim the interest. Higher rate taxpayers will owe extra tax. The position regarding insurance-based products varies – you should check this out for yourself.

Unit trusts

Unit trusts have become an increasingly popular way of investing, particularly for small investors willing to commit part of their savings to something other than entirely risk-free areas.

A unit trust is a fund of money which is then invested in a number of equities on the stock markets of the world. You participate by buying a number of units, and benefit both from the trust's judicious spread of investment and from its professional management of the portfolio of shares, thus reducing the risk which you might otherwise run if you held a few direct shareholdings.

Tightly regulated by the Department of Trade and Industry, and now by the Securities and Investments Board and by the trustee who actually holds the shares, unit trusts will rarely make you a fortune. However, they should not drop as dramatically as an individual share could if the market falls.

Unit trust managers are required to make clear the objectives of each unit trust. Some funds concentrate on a particular industry, e.g. technology, or a particular country, e.g. Japan, or they may have a general selection. Some aim for maximum capital growth but a low income, in which case you may be recommended to have 'accumulation' units, which means that the income is added to your fund and not paid direct to you. Others are designed to pay a higher income but have the probability of lower capital growth. You will receive a dividend ('distribution') twice a year (in some cases, four times a year). This represents your share of all the dividends received by the trust managers. The managers charge for their work and expertise, but this is built into the daily prices quoted for the unit trust and is reflected in the distribution made.

Some unit trust managers offer monthly income plans, providing a growing level of income as well as some growth in the value of the units. These could make a good home for some of your investments.

The possibilities may seem bewildering, so seek advice before putting money into this type of investment. The Unit Trust Association (address in Appendix 8) will supply free literature to help you find the unit trust to meet your particular requirements. Alternatively your bank or a financial adviser who specializes in unit trusts can provide advice and access.

If you do not have a lump sum to invest but want to save a small amount regularly, some unit trusts offer monthly savings plans. These are very efficient vehicles for regular savings.

Basic rate tax is deducted before you get your income from a unit trust. Non-taxpayers can reclaim this. Higher rate taxpayers will owe extra tax. When you sell your units you may have to pay capital gains tax if you have used up your annual exemption.

Investment trusts
Investment trusts should not be confused with unit trusts. Both invest in stocks and shares of other companies, but an investment trust is a public company and if you invest with them you buy shares in the company itself and not in the value of the shares held. This does, of course, give you an interest in all the companies in which the trust itself holds shares. The managers buy and sell investments on the world's stock markets. Capital gains made are not distributed in cash, but are used to increase the value of the trust's assets and, since the number of shares is fixed, the asset value per share therefore increases. As a shareholder you are entitled to a share of the dividend and a say in the way it is run. Investment trusts also offer savings plans.

The Association of Investment Trust Companies (address in Appendix 8) produces literature on how investment trusts work, and also statistics on their investment performance.

Basic rate income tax is deducted from your dividend from an investment trust. Non-taxpayers can reclaim tax. Higher rate taxpayers will owe extra tax. If you sell your shares at a profit you may be liable for capital gains tax.

Stocks and shares
Ownership of stocks and shares has increased dramatically in recent years, boosted by the government's privatization programmes and the general encouragement given to be part of the share-owning democracy.

Unfortunately people don't always realize that prices can go down as well as up, sometimes with alarming speed and severity – as we saw in October 1987! So although there is potential for you to make a small fortune on the stock market, you could just as easily lose out.

Never put into stocks and shares money you are likely to need at short notice or of which you can't afford to lose some if things go wrong. Always take sound advice or buy shares in companies about which you have some genuine personal knowledge.

Money has to be invested through a stockbroker. Since the main London stockbrokers nowadays tend to prefer to invest large sums, it isn't as easy as it used to be to find someone to deal in small amounts, although some banks offer share-buying services. There is also an increasing number of share shops. The Public Information Department of the International Stock Exchange (address in Appendix 8), has a wide range of literature and will provide names and addresses of stockbrokers throughout the country who offer services to the small private investor.

Stockbrokers' commissions vary, not only from one firm to another but also for different types of transaction, so find out first what it is going to cost you to buy or sell shares. On the first £7,000 you spend, commission is 1·25 per cent to 1·65 per cent (usually plus VAT). It is less on larger amounts. The minimum charge is likely to be £10 to £20. There is also stamp duty of 0·5 per cent to pay, and 80p contract levy if the transaction is higher than £1,000. When you sell shares, commission and contract levy are payable at the same rates.

A final word of advice: don't ever be tempted into buying shares in companies you have never heard of on the strength of persuasive telephone calls, letters or callers at the door. The investment world is full of sad stories of people who bought shares on a hot tip from a stranger who telephoned them, only to find that very soon afterwards the stranger and their money both disappeared. Don't risk being a victim – send such salesmen packing, or at least carefully check their credentials before talking to them. Then, too, there are unsolicited approaches from impressive-sounding firms on the mainland of Europe that have turned out to be very doubtful prospects. Ask your bank manager for advice – he will often be able to tell you the real value of some of the so-called inside information and of the offers supposedly specially set aside for you, or to tell you where to make further enquiries.

Basic rate income tax is deducted from dividends before distribution. Non-taxpayers can reclaim; higher rate taxpayers will owe extra. Profits when you sell could be liable to capital gains tax.

Insurance-linked investments
There are many types of insurance-linked investments for regular
savings and lump sum investments. Viewed purely as investments,
they tend to be on the cautious side. If you have an insurance-
linked scheme started before the 1984 Budget, you will be enjoying some tax relief on your premiums.

Be careful if you do not want to commit your money for long
periods. Some of the conventional insurance savings schemes,
such as endowment assurance policies, are entirely satisfactory for
some, but not for those who need ready access to their capital.

Buy only from reputable companies which are in the Association of British Insurers (ABI) or through members of one of the
new Self-Regulatory Organizations, such as the Financial Intermediaries, Managers and Brokers Regulatory Association (FIM-
BRA) and the Life Assurance and Unit Trust Regulatory Organisation (LAUTRO).

Never buy life assurance on impulse. Make quite sure you know
what you are going into, and that it really is right for you. Always
try to get competitive quotations before deciding on a particular
scheme. Shop around and compare like with like.

New types of savings and investment options
There are increasing numbers of new options available. If you are
on the adventurous side, ask about them. Two of the most
popular are outlined below.

Business expansion scheme. This aims to encourage investment in
the shares of certain companies. They are usually new and small
businesses which are not quoted on the stock markets. The BES
allows you tax relief at your top rate of tax on your investments
up to a ceiling of £40,000 each year. In order to qualify you
normally have to keep the shares in the company for five years.
This is not really for the novice investor who wants to do his own
thing, but can be very useful to the fledgling company and
profitable for the investor if things work out as intended.

Personal equity plans. These, called PEPs, are designed to encourage first-time shareholders. You can invest up to £3,000 a
year in shares through an authorized plan manager. You get the
dividends and any profits free of income tax and capital gains tax.
But you have to keep your money in the PEP until at least the

end of the year following the year when you started to invest.
Each year you can invest in only one PEP, but you can choose a
different plan each year. There are also ways in which you can
invest in PEPs via unit trusts.

Again, these are not for the novice investor who isn't too sure
of her tax position, but they are well worth considering when you
have had some experience of investing.

GETTING FINANCIAL ADVICE

An important point to remember in relation to savings and
investment is that you must know who you are dealing with and
make sure she/he knows your circumstances.

The vast majority of us will recognize that as far as finance is
concerned, and in particular savings and investment, we are babes
in the wood! If we have decided we need a financial adviser,
where do we turn and how do we choose?

The chances are that a horde of financial advisers will find you,
so you won't have to look very hard or very long. Your problem
is, and always will be, finding the right one to deal with your
business.

First, though, why is personal finance suddenly so prominent a
matter? Today millions of £s are being spent promoting each of
the major players in the market, the insurance companies, the
banks, the building societies, the unit trust management companies. The following figures will show why:

- By 1997 parents who die will leave to their heirs a total of £24
  billion every year (a 240 per cent increase on current levels).
- One in five adults now holds stocks and shares of some kind.
- One in ten adults invests in private health care.

In Appendix 1, you will find details of why the new Financial
Services Act is important and how it will help you. The Act
requires that all advisers are registered, either as independent
(recommending investments from a wide range of different companies' products) or as company representatives (selling from a
single company's range of products). You should check this point
before you deal with them. That section also spells out what
financial advisers are, what they offer and the bases on which they
charge.

LOOKING FOR FINANCIAL SERVICES AND ADVICE

Choosing your financial adviser is something that only you can do.
Here is a list of things to consider when you are trying to reach a
decision. If you take these into account you will feel confident
that you are making the right choice.

Factors to consider

- Reputation of the organization concerned. Qualifications of
  staff – top level and working level
- Size and stability of company
- Range of services
- Level of investor protection
- Membership of professional and self-regulatory bodies
- Cost advantages – including 'free' services
- Convenience to you in terms of location and business hours
- Unusual services – personalized or particularly applicable to
  you
- Flexibility and adaptability to your needs
- Quick service from polite and approachable staff
- How they treat women

YOUR AT-A-GLANCE GUIDE TO INVESTMENTS

We have emphasized that before you make any decision about
savings and investment you must make sure that you thoroughly
consider all the relevant details. The checklist which follow offers
you a starting-point for easy reference.

Investments checklist

Fixed returns, capital secure

- Banks (fixed term, fixed rate deposit accounts), building society fixed rate bonds, gilts, income and growth bonds and local
  authority loans, National Savings Certificates and Yearly Plan

Variable returns, capital secure

- Banks and building society deposit accounts, national savings
  investment accounts and income and deposit bonds

Inflation-proof (for savings and/or income)

- Index-linked investments, including index-linked issues of
  National Savings Certificates and index-linked government
  stock (gilts)

Capital growth (with risk)
● Business expansion scheme, gilts, unit and investment trusts, personal equity plans and stocks and shares

Regular income (monthly)
● Banks, building societies, national savings income bonds and unit trusts

For regular savings
● Banks, building societies, National Savings Yearly Plan, unit trusts, investment trusts

A WORD ABOUT ANNUITIES

When you buy an annuity, you pay an insurance company a lump sum, and it pays you in return a regular income until you die. The income you receive is dependent on many factors, including your age and your sex. The income you get will be fixed at the time you buy the annuity and the higher the current interest rates are, the higher your income will be.

There are several types of annuity. You will need to check out the type which satisfies your need, and to consider your tax position. Home income plans are one way of converting the capital value of your home to provide you with an income.

There are also variations of a basic system in which your home can be used as the equivalent of the lump sum in exchange for annual or other regular payments and, often, a useful one-off cash payment as well. This is rather like a mortgage in reverse. See Section 11 for more details. Do remember two points:

● With some plans, when you die your home will belong to the financial institution which paid your annuity.
● With all annuities, the longer you live the more profitable the scheme is for you.

SUMMARY

● If you have money to save or invest it is important to know what you want from it – income or growth.
● There is no shortage of advice – in this book you will find signposting to help you find it.
● Only you can diagnose what is right for your own particular circumstances. Make sure that you give enough time and care to this.

- Decisions about saving and investing are based on a comparison of the different options available to you, what the level of return is likely to be and what the level of risk is that you will be called upon to take.
- Having decided on the type of scheme that suits you, shop around for quotes. Be especially cautious about unsolicited offers.
- A vital consideration is your tax position: this will make a difference to the attractiveness of the options. There is no set rule as everyone's situation is unique.

Section 13

Setting up in business and running a small business

INTRODUCTION

If you are like many women, you will find that every now and then you have an idea which you think is particularly appropriate for development into a business of your own.

Perhaps you are intrigued with the idea of being your own boss, and having the excitement of running your own business. You would like to have your own business, but you don't know how to set about things. What do you need to know?

This section will outline the key factors you should consider before you take any decision. It will then guide you through the various stages so that you can decide whether or not your idea is a practical proposition – and if it is, what to do about it.

Today more and more women (and men as well) find that being their own boss is an attractive idea. It could be a wise move for you to make if you have the skills, stamina and discipline necessary to make the system work for you. You will need to be practical and realistic from the word 'Go'. Reading this section should keep your feet on the ground. If you do decide to go ahead with setting up a business and running it, you will experience a maximum of excitement and satisfaction and hopefully a minimum of the frustration and worry that can be involved.

KEY FACTORS

We start with you. You must know what you have to bring to a new venture: no one else is involved in the decision at this stage. You have to decide on your capability to start and run your own business. Having a gut feeling that you can do it and that you are a budding entrepreneur is useful, but it isn't enough. You must be firmly realistic with yourself at this stage, remembering that all market places are intensely competitive. The rewards of success can be great but the costs of failure can be catastrophic, and you need to know what you are doing from the outset.

Who can help you at this stage?
Discussing the possibility with friends and relations can help, but it can also hinder. Their reaction won't, after all, be unbiased.

Discussing the matter with someone like your bank manager or someone else who may eventually lend you money can help. But it is important not to ask someone in a professional capacity to help you think out what may, at this point, be a raw and incomplete concept. That would destroy their confidence in you, and you need their confidence for later on.

Here is a list of questions which you should answer honestly to clear your mind about your own position.

- Why do you want to start a business?
- Have you had this urge for a long time or is it new to you?
- What is new, useful and worthwhile about your concept?
- Do you honestly believe that there is room for this new business in your community? Why?
- What expertise do you have (or can you get) for the business that is better than other people's?
- How energetic are you?
- Can you work long hours?
- Do you give up easily?
- When you start things, do you continue with them and finally finish them?
- Can you cope with the worry and insecurity of running a business?
- What would you do if you had to borrow money for the business against your personal and family assets, such as your home, your pension or your life savings?
- Will your family and/or friends support you, or could your responsibilities to them create conflicts?
- How good are you at personal money management? Could you cope with the complex money management needed for a business?
- Are you a self-confident or a timid person?
- Can you take criticism?
- Can you plan effectively?
- Are you self-disciplined?

- How much real knowledge and/or experience will you bring to the venture regarding the products or services you will be dealing with? Do you know the market? Do you understand marketing and promotion? (You can consult experts on some of these, but you must understand the issues in order to find and direct the right experts.)
- Do you know what you don't know (most important)?
- How good are you at administration and delegation?
- How good is your health? (Sir John Harvey Jones, former chairman of ICI, has identified good health and physical stamina as most important factors for success in business.)

When you have looked at the answers you have given to these questions, you will know whether or not you stand a chance of being successful in starting and running your own business.

In just as much detail, you should now examine other factors. These include:

- Your own skills in the areas of finance, marketing and management.
- The concept you have for your new business. You need to be sure you have defined and refined this, and that you have done enough background research to decide whether there is a niche which you can fill.
- Your future potential customers: who they are, how many of them there are and how you will reach them.
- Your future competitors: who they are, how many of them there are, how long established they are, how they operate and the degree of success they have.
- Whether you have access to the type of finance and other resources and/or help you need to make a successful entry into the market place.

YOUR POSSIBLE NEW VENTURE
You now need to decide on the profile of your new venture.

Every business has its own 'personality', which evolves all the time. Try to think of the new business as a person. What sort of person is it? Young or old? High-tech or friendly and cosy? Super-efficient or warm and practical? A man or woman – or possibly asexual!

The next important factor is that of reputation. Right from the word 'Go' your new business will have a reputation. You will be communicating about it all the time – even if you don't know it. Communication is not simply a matter of making a particular point when you write a letter or place an advertisement in the local paper; it is ongoing. Even during the time you are considering setting up a new business you are communicating about it, and it is gaining – or losing – reputation.

The watchword is 'be careful' all the time, even before you have taken a decision to go ahead.

YOUR OPTIONS
In basic terms these are:

- To become self-employed, operating as a sole trader
- To set up in partnership with one or more others
- To set up a limited company.

There are, of course, pros and cons for each of the options, and within each there may be variants. You may, for example, be interested in operating a franchise for some other well-established organization. You may wish to start a completely new venture of your own, in an entirely new area. Or you may be interested in something in between the two.

Self-employed/sole trader
Running your own business as a sole trader is simple – you don't have any legal formalities and you will not be required to have your accounts audited, although that is advisable. The business is all yours – but do remember that its debts are all yours too. If you get into trouble you could lose the roof over your head. If you decide to go into business by yourself, tell the Inland Revenue, the DHSS, and also your local authority, and check whether the business area in which you will be operating requires you to take out a licence or seek planning permission or other legal authority. When you have got the business established and running you should check whether you need to register for VAT.

There are many small businesses operating happily and successfully as sole traders.

Partnerships
Working as a partnership can be very similar to working as a sole trader in that there are no external legal formalities. You simply decide to work with one or more others. This may be sufficient

for starting the new venture, but it is businesslike to enter into a partnership agreement once you know that the business has a future. To do this you will need to consult a solicitor. With a partnership agreement all partners will know where they stand. The profits will be shared as agreed, generally in proportion to the money or business brought in by each partner. Remember, though, that each partner is responsible for all the debts of the partnership, and that your home could be forfeit. The lesson is – choose your partner(s) with great care.

Again, there are many small businesses operating as happy and growing partnerships.

Limited company

A limited company has its own legal existence, quite separate and distinct from the people who own it and from those who run it. This is where the main advantage lies. If the company runs into financial or other problems, you have a measure of protection. The law, though, has developed in recent years and the obligations on directors of a limited company are now much stricter than they used to be. This is an area where you need to do your homework very thoroughly before you make a decision. There are legal and accountancy costs involved and a raft of procedures to be followed to comply with formalities such as registering the company with the Companies Registration Office (Department of Trade), auditing and filing the company accounts each year, etc. The Institute of Directors publishes useful guides to the responsibilities of company directors, which are considerable.

Having said all that, don't be put off if you really believe in the potential for your new business. Think about consulting an accountant; many will give a preliminary consultation free of charge and without obligation. A competent accountant can give advice that determines whether you succeed or fail.

Other types of businesses

Franchise operations

You could decide to buy a franchise. This will enable you to sell the franchise company's products or services, using its name, company logo, experience, guidance and often its supplies and materials, etc. This is an increasingly popular choice today. Many well-known High Street businesses are franchises: Wimpy,

Kentucky Fried Chicken, Dyno-Rod and even some hotels are examples. You can trade as a sole trader, a partnership or a limited company.

Cooperatives

The cooperative is another and different sort of business. Everyone involved shares responsibilities for the decisions, the rewards and the problems. You can operate as an ordinary limited company or have limited liability by being registered under the Industrial and Provident Societies Act.

FACTS OF LIFE IN RELATION TO SMALL BUSINESSES

The benefits of starting and running a small business are that you can make money, you will have a job, you could find you are creating jobs for others and you should be able to get a lot of personal satisfaction out of what you are achieving and the lifestyle you are enjoying. You will not be doing what your boss wants; you will be the boss. You will be serving your business instead, and many entrepreneurs enjoy just this.

On the other hand, there are factors to remember which are less attractive. They include the risk of losing money, the possibility of never being able to call your time your own, being at the beck and call of your customers and your employees, lots and lots of work and lots and lots of worry when things aren't going as you would wish them to go.

GOING AHEAD – THE FIRST STEPS

Let's assume you've decided to go ahead. You now need to get down to some serious planning. The path is well identified and there are many ways in which you can get help when you need it. But it is important that you think your position out for yourself before you try to fill in the blanks by getting information, advice and help from others.

THE BUSINESS PLAN

You should start with the preparation of a business plan. This is important for many reasons, including the following:

- To keep you on a straight course in relation to the development of the business. You must know where you are going, whether you are on the right path and whether you are in danger of

being diverted from it.
- To give you confidence that you have planned adequately and have the ability to manage your new enterprise.
- To demonstrate to yourself – and others – that there is a market for the product or service you will be introducing, and that you are going about things the right way.
- To have something to show to those from whom you may be trying to get help, in terms of joining you in the enterprise, lending you money or buying the goods or services you will be selling.

It is important to write the business plan down. Its various elements include:
- The definition of the business
- Its objectives
- The strategy to be used to achieve the objectives
- The plan of operation
- The financial plan
- Planning for the future.

We shall now look at some of those elements in detail.

Setting objectives
This is a matter of putting down on paper the four or five aims of the business. Here is an example:

- The business is to be:
  – A small, effective secretarial office and business centre facility in a small town.
- The basic objective is:
  – To establish XYZ Ltd as providers of quality business services in Borchester.
- Some early objectives include:
  – To identify the services on offer – secretarial, photocopying, fax, telex, design and graphic and print.
  – To underline the cost-effective nature of the services by comparison with competitors in the area.
  – To identify the company's 'unique sales proposition' – twenty-four-hour service, office or home delivery and money-back guarantee if not satisfied.
  – To underline that this is a family business of principals and family members.

The strategy

This will set out the way in which the objectives will be achieved. It should detail how the personality of the business will be established and the way in which the marketing will be carried out and the message got across, in broad terms. For example, it will:

- Identify and quantify the exact market.
- Identify and secure the resources required (such as office, staff, expertise, finance, publicity).
- Identify and watch the competition and avoid or collaborate with or overcome it as appropriate.
- Plan for development of the business, in particular with regard to your own role in the business.

The operational plan

This should cover the details of the business and its market place and include a survey of the competition. It should give details of why the product or service is unique and/or better than the competition, and of the means for profiting from this. It should set out how the business will operate, covering its management, any relevant patents or other intellectual properties, and it should also include information about the potential customers of the business – who they are, how they will buy and above all how they will be paying for the product or service.

Details of selling, promotion and marketing should be included, with possible costs of staff, commission, production of literature and advertising material, and also the cost of space in publications or broadcast media.

Operational details should include where the business will be based, whether in freehold or leasehold premises, equipment needed and so on. To summarize, operational details cover who does what, how, to whom and with what reward.

The financial plan

This should include as much detail as possible in the following areas:

- Sales and costs forecasts
- Resources required and how they will be paid for
- Monthly cash flow forecasts, for at least twelve months

- Monthly profit and loss forecasts, for at least twelve months
- Profit forecasts for five years
- Forecast balance sheet for first and second year
- Assumptions behind the forecasts
- Information on risks which could affect the business, steps to be taken to avoid them and measures to cope with disappointments and disasters.

Planning for the future

Here again, you need to include as much information as you possibly can. It should be in relation to:

- Your long-term objectives for the business, say over five years.
- An estimate of resources needed, in terms of finance, premises, equipment and man/woman power.
- Your concept of the business structure over the period (whether or not you may need to increase the capital in the business, the number of shareholders, etc.).
- Your view of the prospects for the people/organizations investing in your business, working with you as colleagues/ shareholders/employees, buying from you as customers or liaising with you as suppliers.
- Your needs at the time of retirement and later in life (for a pension, etc.).

PRESENTING YOUR BUSINESS PLAN

Having written your business plan, you will need to review it in relation to whom you will be presenting it to. This will depend on the nature and scale of your new business. For some modest finance or overdraft facilities to start up, a paper covering the points above, a few pages long, will do as a discussion document for an appointment with your bank manager. If, however, you want to raise a significant sum of money, say £50,000 or over, you will need to go into the matter in much more detail, with detailed facts and figures. Most of the clearing banks have good information kits which will help you to understand how to start up in business. In many cases these are related to the specific services they offer to new businesses. Get as many of the different kits as you can and spend time discovering just what is on offer, both from the banks and from the government. We are living in an age of enterprise. Ensure it works for you, not against you.

Most accountants can advise on the sources of finance available, on who is most likely to provide finance and on how to present your plan in the most favourable way. Many accountants work closely with lenders of widely varying amounts.

ENTERPRISE ALLOWANCE

You could qualify for an Enterprise Allowance to help you set up a new business of your own. You must be receiving Unemployment Benefit or Income Support when you apply and have been without work for at least eight weeks. In addition, you must have £1,000 to invest in your business (this does not have to be in the form of cash; an agreement for a loan from a bank or a relative would qualify).

The Enterprise Allowance is currently £40 a week for a year, which is paid in addition to what you earn. You can get free help and advice from your local Enterprise Agency, the Small Firms Service and the Scottish or Welsh Development Agencies. Free business training and even free banking are also available to you within the scheme. Your Jobcentre will give you full details.

RUNNING A SMALL BUSINESS

Most of the principles for starting your own business apply to running a small business. If you are already doing just that, you will already have learned some of the lessons! Check up on what you know and, as said previously, do recognize what you don't know and make up your mind to learn and find out what is necessary.

Running an established business offers you the benefits of existing customers and suppliers, and established premises, equipment and staff. The possibility of joining a business which you will have the opportunity of running, or even buying or taking over, can be an attractive prospect.

There are several important aspects for you to check carefully. An accountant should be able to advise you about them. They include:

- *Location.* Is it good? Is there adequate access, car-parking, traffic?
- *Potential.* Can you genuinely expect to increase turnover and profit? Is there likely to be increased competition?

- *Business*. Is the reputation good and/or capable of being improved? Are systems adequate? Is information up to date?
- *Price*. Is it reasonable? Is it worth it?
- *Equipment, buildings, stock*. Do these represent value for money?
- *Staff*. Are these satisfactory? Will they prove helpful in the new situation? Are wages/salaries reasonable?

SUMMARY

- If you want to set up in business it is important:
  - to know yourself
  - to be sure of what you have to offer, the potential market and your competition
  - to take practical steps and write the business plan
  - to assess the levels of time, determination and commitment you must give to your new enterprise
  - having decided to go ahead, to do just that.
- If you want to continue to run a small business, you should also take time to check your current position and to plan thoughtfully for the future.
- Talk to banks about their services and get their information packs in relation to setting up and running small businesses.
- You should recognize where the sources of help are, so that you can turn to them when you need help, advice and, if necessary, finance.

Section 14

Financial planning for retirement

INTRODUCTION

It is a striking but perhaps unsurprising fact that, despite a decade of movement towards greater equality for women at work, only a small amount of progress has been made towards encouraging women to make as much provision for a pension as their male counterparts.

Because most women have the role of wife and mother, substantial numbers prefer, or find it necesssary, to work part-time. This, in many cases, excludes them from direct participation in their company's occupational pension scheme. Even where she is allowed to participate, a woman frequently finds that the same annual pension contribution for the same job as her male colleague provides her with less pension when she retires because her working life is commonly shorter. In virtually every final salary scheme two people on the same pay build up the same pension each year, but a person who only works for twenty years won't build up as big a pension overall as a person who works for thirty to forty years. A pension company's response to any enquiry about a pension for a woman usually gives the cost of a woman's earlier retirement age and her greater life expectancy as an explanation of why her pension would be expected to be less than that of a man in the same employment situation.

In the past many women have been able to rely on their husbands' state and occupational pensions. Today the security of this is reduced because of the greater likelihood of couples being divorced late in married life. In relation to state benefits, a woman in this situation should calculate her husband's contributions up to the date of the divorce and have these applied to her own benefit in due course. This matter should be discussed with your local DHSS office.

This section:

- Outlines briefly the extent to which women provide for their retirement at present.

- Explains how you, as a woman currently at work, can plan for
  the future. This covers the following situations:
  - being employed or self-employed
  - working for an employer who provides a pension scheme or
    one who does not
  - your rights if you work part-time
  - being contracted in or out of the state earnings-related pen-
    sion scheme (SERPS).

A full explanation is given of the new pension structure created
by the Social Security Act 1986; most of the changes under that
Act are being implemented during 1988. In particular, attention
will be focused on the potential advantages and disadvantages of
the new personal pension plans which employees have had the
right to take out since July 1988.

A WOMAN AND PENSIONS TODAY

Until recently, a common assumption has been that where only
one partner in a marriage is providing the pension it is bound to
be the man. This has led to a number of unsatisfactory results.

Only one-third of retired women receive a full basic state
pension in their own right from their own national insurance
contributions. Up to 2 million women who have worked at some
point in their lives have no entitlement to any pension in their
own right and instead have to wait until their husband retires
before he can then claim the married man's pension (which is
substantially lower than two single people's pensions). This is
because many women decide to pay reduced married women's
national insurance contributions – an option which fortunately has
not been available since 1978 except for those who were paying at
the reduced rate before that date. Those who have not paid full
contributions, even if they are significantly older than their husbands, will not receive any pension at all until their husband
retires at 65.

A partial explanation of the situation is that more women than
men have not pursued full-time careers, particularly in the group
of women who are currently retired. Another explanation is that
women have been more likely to work in non-pensionable employment or in part-time work (where pension provisions are less
common). These are factors which are gradually being eroded
over time.

More worrying, a substantial number of women have had the option to join their employers' pension schemes but have in the past turned it down. Frequently this initial decision not to join an employer's scheme has been irreversible even though it may have later been regretted.

Even where a husband's occupational scheme appears to provide adequately for a couple's retirement needs, this may continue to be adequate only while the husband is alive. Although current law allows pension providers to pay a widow's pension at up to two-thirds of the married rate, most schemes pay 50 per cent and a few pay as little as 25 per cent. Couples may believe that they have planned adequately for their retirement, but they may overlook the fact that they will be satisfactorily provided for only for as long as they both jointly survive.

When you do provide yourself with an occupational pension, this is frequently on less favourable terms than those usually available to your husband or partner. Thus, while 99 per cent of men's occupational pension schemes give the widow a pension, the proportion of schemes for women which give a pension to the widower is very much lower. This is extraordinary and it reflects the social prejudice that a man should provide for his wife in retirement but not vice versa. A woman who wants to provide for her husband has an option to do so in most schemes, but only very few of them take it up.

One thing to watch out for if you get divorced and your husband finds a new partner is that he is likely to change his 'expression of wish' document in favour of his new partner. In the event of his death his lump sum life assurance benefit will go to his new partner, not to you, his former wife. As a divorced wife you may, therefore, be left with few if any pension rights unless you take steps to correct the matter.

CONSIDERATIONS FOR WOMEN PLANNING A PENSION

The above points will neither help nor console you if you are already on a low or non-existent pension, but they do provide some guidance for you if you are currently at work. You need to know what to watch out for when planning your future pension. In particular you can identify some of the pitfalls to avoid. A number of points are worth bearing in mind:

1. In the past many women have not had adequate pensions, partly the result of ingrained and unrealized prejudices in

society in this area of financial provision, and partly the result of the attitude of women themselves. The DHSS system which operated up to 1978, under which married women could deprive themselves of pension rights through paying the married women's reduced rate national insurance contribution, was a major factor. Once married couples are taxed separately, from April 1990, the situation should change. Even so, it is likely to be a long drawn-out process.

2. Women are disadvantaged by the types of employment they are more likely to take on; these often provide no occupational pension scheme or have schemes with unfavourable conditions attached.

3. Both state and occupational pensions rely on many years' contributions (often 40) to build them up to the maximum. Even career women are likely to have missed some years of the contributions required for a maximum pension, and they are likely to have worked in several different jobs. They are therefore unlikely to have maximum benefits in any scheme.

4. The rise in the divorce rate makes it more likely than ever before that women relying on their husbands for a pension will lose some or all of their previously expected benefits when a divorce occurs. If you are contemplating a possible divorce, consult a solicitor to ensure you don't lose out in relation to pension and/or death benefits.

MAKE YOUR OWN PENSION PROVISION

Not having a pension in your own right places you in an extremely vulnerable position, whether you are single or married. If you are at work it is essential that you should consider what pension provisions you want and know how to go about achieving them. Numerous changes being brought about during 1988 affect the pension scene; much of the extra choice available may benefit working women more than men. The details below explain what is on offer and what considerations should be borne in mind in pension planning.

THE PRESENT PENSION POSITION

At present there are a number of possible ways in which you as a member of the working population can make provision for your pension. The government's changes aim to give employees more choice and more scope for future planning, regardless of their present employer.

The two state schemes

The flat rate scheme
This is the original simple state pension scheme, introduced in the late 1940s at the same time as the general introduction of the current system of national insurance benefits and contributions.

It results in a flat-rate pension for which those women who have paid the appropriate number of contributions qualify; the amount is £41.15 per week from April 1988. Most women who have recently retired have not completed the necessary forty years' full contributions and are therefore likely to receive only a proportion of this amount. Many married women now retiring may not qualify for any pension; if they have paid the married women's reduced rate of contributions they have no entitlement. The current pension (from April 1988) is £2,139 a year for a single person, plus an additional £1,287 for an adult dependant or non-working wife who does not have her own state pension. The pension rises annually in line with increases in the retail price index.

The state earnings-related pension scheme
Since 1978, most working women should have been building up contributions towards a basic pension and many will also have been paying contributions towards the state earnings-related pension scheme (SERPS), unless they were a member of a 'contracted out' occupational pension scheme, as explained later. The aim of SERPS (until modified recently) has been to provide an extra annual pension of between 1·25 per cent and 25 per cent (depending on income) of the average of your earnings revalued in line with average national earnings. The 25 per cent adds up to a little below one-quarter of average annual earnings as income below the national insurance lower earnings limit (£2,132 in 1988) is excluded. Earnings above the maximum contribution limit are also excluded because revaluation is based on average national earnings and not individual earnings.

SERPS aims to top up people's pensions to an amount which reflects their earnings when they were employed. However, neither this nor the basic state pension is likely to provide you with a lavish retirement pension. For this reason, and also because of the obvious tax incentives, many employers have also provided occupational pension schemes.

Occupational pension schemes

There are a large number of schemes which will be outlined below, but the essential advantage of occupational pension schemes is that contributions are allowable as a tax-free expense for the employer. They also qualify the employee for income tax relief. All income and capital gains in a pension fund are tax-free and so, too, are lump sums paid on retirement. However, the quid pro quo for all these reliefs is that money in the fund is not available to you until you reach retirement age.

Here are some examples to give an idea of the range of the schemes.

Contributory and non-contributory schemes

- *Contributory schemes.* In these both the employer and the employee contribute towards the scheme. Often on changing employment your pension becomes frozen until retirement, instead of the transfer value being passed on to the new employer. That can lead to reduced total benefits at retirement. It is best to join a scheme which allows you to take a worthwhile transfer value with you to put into a scheme with your new employer.
- *Non-contributory schemes.* In these the employer makes all the contributions. Sometimes you may be able to take a transfer value, but often there is a considerable penalty on changing employers.

Compulsory and voluntary schemes

These have important differences. Before April 1988 some employers' schemes were voluntarily open to those who were invited to participate. You were able to choose whether to belong to the scheme.

Other schemes were compulsory; you had to belong. They have often had a major disadvantage for the short-term employee who stayed in a job for up to five years: all pension rights could be lost on leaving the job.

Defined benefit or defined contribution schemes

These also have important differences. All company pension schemes are either defined benefit or defined contribution schemes. A defined benefit scheme is one in which employees receive defined benefits regardless of the performance of money (their contributions) invested in the scheme. Usually the benefits are one-sixtieth or one-eightieth of final pay for every year in the scheme. Defined contribution schemes are ones in which contributions from the employer and/or the employee are at defined rates with the ultimate value of the pension depending upon what the value of the fund at retirement will purchase. These are more commonly known as money-purchase schemes or with-profits schemes.

Contracted-in and contracted-out schemes

Some employers have contracted-out schemes. This means that the pension provision of the scheme is a substitute for SERPS (though in some cases the pension may be smaller), and consequently the DHSS allows both contracted-out employers and employees to pay the lower rate of national insurance contributions. This automatically takes that company's employees out of participation in the SERPS scheme. These contracted-out schemes have until April 1988 been defined benefit schemes, but since then defined contribution schemes can also be contracted out.

Where a scheme is contracted in, its participants will be entitled to SERPS benefits as well as those of their company pension scheme when they retire. They and their employers will pay the full rate of national insurance contributions.

One of the most contentious parts of arrangements in the past has been that whether an employer's scheme is voluntary or compulsory, an employee has not been allowed to set up any other pension arrangement once she has joined the company scheme. As already indicated, this has been a major hindrance to those changing jobs frequently and also to those who plan substantial breaks from work in their careers.

Generally employees have had little or no choice in their own pension arrangements. They have had to accept what they were entitled to and what they paid for (if anything), and then plan any compensating extra benefits for retirement by means such as investments, life assurance or additional voluntary contributions to an employer's scheme (if available).

Until recently the only individuals who have been able to set up pension plans outside a company scheme have been the self-employed and those not in company schemes. The essential principle of these personal pension schemes is similar to a money purchase scheme. Contributions are linked with an insurance policy during the individual's career and then, on retirement, an annuity is purchased to provide a pension. These schemes have been the only means of extra pension provision for the self-employed, who cannot participate in SERPS. They have been of much less value for an employee without a company pension as if she or he changed jobs to a firm with a compulsory pension scheme, they have had to discontinue contributions. The policy is preserved, the money already paid in remaining invested until retirement.

REFORMING THE PENSION SYSTEM
The present government has been determined to reform the pension system for two reasons.

1. First, it wishes to give greater choice to all employees so that they are not forced to join company schemes on disadvantageous terms and so that pensions are not a hindrance to decisions to change employment.
2. Secondly, it wishes to shift the emphasis of earnings-related pension provision from the SERPS scheme to greater personal provision for pension needs (note that personal pensions are not earnings related). This is in no small part because an ageing population has caused the projected cost of SERPS to increase substantially over that originally expected when it was set up in 1978.

In order to meet their objectives, the government has made several changes, which came into force on 1 July 1988.

1. It is now no longer compulsory for you to be a member of a company pension scheme. This will apply both to new employees and to existing employees – they no longer have to remain members.
2. If you elect not to participate in a company pension scheme you can set up your own personal pension plan. If this is an

'appropriate personal pension plan' it will entitle you to pay the contracted-out rate of national insurance contributions. Contracted-out personal pensions are subject to a number of restrictions.

3. All company pension schemes must offer facilities for additional voluntary contributions (AVCs) to their own scheme so that as an employee you can buy extra pension. You are also allowed to make freestanding AVCs to a pension scheme other than the one operated by your own company. This again means you can enhance your pension benefits. The AVC facility should be particularly useful to you if you have been with your company scheme for only a short part of your working life and are now nearing retirement. It will also be useful if you have had significant career breaks.

4. If you are self-employed you will be in a similar position to that before the changes, except that if you are newly self-employed you will have to take out a self-employed personal pension plan as old-style self-employed retirement annuity contracts are no longer available (but you can continue contributions to an existing policy).

5. In order to encourage everyone to make more use of the new facilities (and to reduce costs) the benefits of the SERPS scheme will be significantly reduced for all those retiring from March 2000 onwards. For those retiring after March 2010 SERPS will be further reduced, making it unattractive for most employees compared with what they could provide by other means. The older an employee is, the better SERPS is.

With regard to personal pensions, it is important to bear in mind the following disadvantages in comparison with most company pension schemes:

- Cover for dependants on death is automatic with most company schemes. To provide benefits at a similar level will require a higher contribution to a personal pension plan.
- The proportion of money swallowed up in expenses will be higher in a personal pension than a company pension.
- Many company schemes actually subsidize people who retire early; early retirement terms under a personal pension plan will be determined on purely commercial terms.

- Even where there is no guarantee, many company schemes have a good track record of paying discretionary increases during retirement. Under a personal pension plan the bigger the rate of increase you require, the smaller the level at which your pension will start.

PENSION CHOICES – THE FUTURE FOR WOMEN

It is obvious from the description above that in future all women will have a greater choice of what they can do about pensions. Their decisions will, in very substantial part, depend upon how long they have been participating in any form of company scheme and, of course, upon their present ages. Those who are youngest, or who have been working for only a short period for their present employer, will have the most free hand. For some a decision on whether or not to leave a company scheme will require detailed financial counselling; for many in the older age groups there may be a definite advantage in not changing.

Younger women

If you are a younger woman starting your career, you have several options. Bear the following points in mind:

- It will not always be the case, even for 20-year-olds, that a personal pension plan is better than an employer's scheme. If a company's pension scheme is fairly generous and, in particular, if it is a money-purchase scheme where the employer makes all or most of the contributions, it may be in the employee's interest to join and/or stay with the company scheme. But do remember that if you find something better, then you can change to it after two years if you are in a final-pay scheme.
- If the company scheme has particularly unfavourable features, such as high contributions, significantly lower pension rates for women paying the same premium as male employees and/or the exclusion of a pension for a widower, then a younger woman may conclude that a personal pension plan is better. In particular, if she expects to take career breaks or to change jobs frequently, a personal scheme may be particularly desirable.
- All company pensions must now provide revaluation of pre-served pensions for those who leave with two or more years'

pensionable service, and they must offer AVC facilities as well
as freestanding AVCs. These might well be significant reasons
for opting for company schemes. Also bear in mind that all
portable personal pension plans will be investment-based
money-purchase schemes, while most companies offer defined
benefit schemes in which the return is more predictable.

If you take the independent route, you or your financial advisers
should consider whether at any particular time your pension
money should be in a deposit type (building society) fund, in a
moderately growing with-profits fund, or in a higher risk unit-
linked insurance company fund (linked to unit trusts). You will
have to decide on your personal attitude to risk/benefit, because
these different types of scheme all have different implications and
your attitude towards risk may change from time to time, according to your circumstances. These are the sorts of choices there is
no need to consider in a defined benefits company scheme because the company is obliged to make up any investment short-
falls that occur.

Older women
Whatever qualms you might feel about your present company's
pension plan, if you are retiring within the next ten to fifteen
years you will almost certainly be better off sticking with your
present company's scheme – particularly if it is contracted in to
SERPS. Even so, you may still be able to make improvements to
your situation through the AVC schemes that all company pension schemes will now have to provide.

THE NEED TO PLAN FOR THE FUTURE
While in the past many women have not provided adequately for
their own pension arrangements, there is no reason to suppose
that this will continue. Certainly it should not. Improvements are
likely for several reasons:

- Some of the past anomalies in the treatment of married women
  are disappearing. In future they will be taxed separately, and
  when working will at least contribute to their own state pensions.
- Company pension schemes which offer unfavourable terms to
  women are likely to disappear by a natural process of commercial attrition; they are no longer compulsory and women in
  companies operating them should desert them in droves.

- Women are gradually becoming far more financially sophisticated. In the younger age group it is increasingly less likely that a wife will be in complete ignorance of her husband's financial affairs. Furthermore, the fact that more and more companies are gradually appointing women at senior positions means that women's interests are likely to be increasingly taken into account.
- The fact that many more women are following careers means that far fewer are likely to be left with a reduced pension of their own and/or half or less of a husband's pension.

It remains true that women are much more likely than men to take career breaks which reduce their pension entitlement and they are, therefore, in danger of underproviding for themselves. In consequence, throughout her working and non-working life before retirement a woman should regularly ask herself:

1. Am I currently building up my pension entitlement? If so, is it enough?
2. Is my company scheme giving me the best deal and, if not, should I consult a financial adviser?
3. If I am self-employed or in non-pensionable employment, should I seek advice about a personal pension plan?
4. If I am married, how different would my pension position be if I were to become divorced, and would it be adequate? Similarly, how different would my position be if my husband died?
5. If I am not working, or if I am taking a career break, how will I provide adequately for my pension later on?

In this way, even if a woman is not always making the pension provision she would like to make, she will at least be aware of exactly where she stands in providing for her retirement pension. If the pension seems likely to be inadequate, she will be able to arrange other assets to bolster her retirement income.

SUMMARY
- Because of the recent changes in legislation, it is vital to know where you stand in relation to your pension on retirement.
- The options are many and complex.
- Remember – it's your retirement, your pension and your money. Make sure that you know enough to make the wisest and most effective decisions, so that you have a retirement free from financial troubles.

Appendix 1

What the new Financial Services Act means to you

Understanding how the new Financial Services Act applies to you is important. It is equally important that you know about the organizations with the responsibility for implementing them (see Appendix 4).

The Act should ensure that you get from your financial advisers, who now must be authorized, what is called 'best advice', and that this best advice is reflected in their 'best execution' of it. In addition it requires that those who are servicing your financial needs must follow what are called the 'know your customer' rules. All these provisions have legal sanction – in the criminal law. If it is proved that you haven't received adequate service, those advising you could end up in jail for a long period of time and never work again as financial advisers. In addition, you should be compensated for any loss suffered.

One of the most important provisions of the Act is for the segregation of clients' money. If you leave funds with a broker other than for immediate investment, they must be kept in a separate account, not be lumped in with the broker's general funds. You must be paid interest on the money unless you have agreed otherwise.

Additionally, the new law lays down that you must know who you are dealing with. The jargon term is 'polarization'; its meaning is that you must be told who is getting financial reward from the business they are writing with you. You should eventually be able to find out a fair amount about the extent of that reward.

Salesmen or advisers have two choices. They can opt for being an agent of a company, employed by that company. You will know that they can sell you only the company's products, which they will naturally seek to promote. Alternatively, they can opt

to be independent advisers, able to study your requirements and
tailor a scheme to suit you. They are paid by the company that
provides the products they end up selling to you, although not all
pay commission. Ensure that you know which sort of representa-
tive you are talking to at any time. In both cases they must deal
with you in line with the provisions of the new Act.

What services can you expect as a result of the new legislation?

SUMMARY OF THE NEW RULES

Best advice
This means that the organization you are dealing with must be
able to prove (if required) that they have conducted a comprehensive check of the many investment options and have put in front
of you relevant options for consideration.

They must have gone into your own circumstances first so they
know what you need and want – see below under 'Know your
customer'.

Best execution
This relates to the manner in which your orders have been
executed. Firms must deal in good time and on the best terms
available. Again, they must work to a comprehensive set of rules.
What they do in practice must conform with the specific rule
books of the Securities and Investment Board and the self-
regulatory organizations.

Know your customer
Fundamentally, this means that your financial circumstances must
be checked so that you are recommended to consider only investments that are suitable for you. You must be made aware of the
level of risk you would be taking before you take the decision to
invest. The adviser must also make sure that you are comfortable
with the risk, understand your commitment and agree to it. This
should help to ensure that the sharks are better controlled in the
future than they have been in the past.

Customer agreement
You must be given a form which sets out the terms and charges
for the business being done.

Uninvited and unsolicited calls

Cold calling is banned, except in relation to life assurance and unit trusts. There are some safeguards in relation to agreements made during cold calls. You are allowed up to fourteen days (twenty-eight in some circumstances) to change your mind and cancel any agreement. The cooling-off period begins with the receipt of a notice informing you of your right to cancel and containing information about the product purchased. There is no cooling-off period if you buy on an execution-only basis or under a customer agreement with an authorized adviser, nor is there any cooling-off period if you make an order by filling in a coupon in an advertisement which contains relevant information about the product.

Appendix 2

Your rights and responsibilities as a customer

In every transaction there are two parties: one is the customer or potential customer, the other is the person or organization from whom the product or service is being purchased. Each has rights and each has responsibilities.

YOUR RIGHTS

As the customer or potential customer, you have the right to have adequate information about the product or service you are thinking of buying; the right to choose; the right to have quality and safety in relation to goods (fitness for purpose); the right to access and the right to redress. These consumer rights have been enshrined in the United Nations.

If, however, you want to have more information than is offered or to complain, bear in mind that there are many ways in which the people you may be dealing with may try to dissuade you. You must be determined and persist if you want results, even if it takes time and money. Of course, you always have the option of settling for a quiet life instead. See Section 10 for guidance on how to complain and get things put right.

YOUR RESPONSIBILITIES

As a consumer you have responsibilities towards those with whom you do business when you buy goods and services. You should remember that their time costs money: you shouldn't waste it. You have a duty to be fair in your dealing with them, to give accurate information and not be irresponsible. Remember, though, that there are many organizations which want to know altogether too much about you. Make sure that none is invading your privacy and asking for more information than they need in relation to the transaction on which you are engaged.

Appendix 3

Who's who in financial services

Here is a simple breakdown of the money managers – who they are and what they offer. They themselves should be your first port of call if you need help and advice. The range of services they provide is becoming wider all the time.

BANKS
Banks offer you general advice and will tell you how to get outside specialist advice.

Some banks are independent advisers; others are representatives. In the main, though, if they are representatives they will have a separate independent financial services organization.

Banks are a good source of advice on management of smaller sums of money. For larger sums (say, over £10,000) you can use the bank's investment arm.

Banks offer many services in the area of investment, ranging from advice on their own products (insurance, unit trusts and personal equity plans, for example) to advice on tax, pensions, stocks and shares, portfolio management, etc.

BUILDING SOCIETIES
Building societies today offer an increasing range of services, as well as the opportunity to buy a house through a mortgage. They, too, now have to decide whether they will be offering independent advice or acting as representatives.

Although most of their activities are in relation to loans and savings accounts, they may also offer share-dealing services and deal in unit trusts.

ACCOUNTANTS AND SOLICITORS
Family accountants and solicitors will generally give you advice on your financial strategy. Some will even offer to manage your investments. Before taking up such an offer, check whether they

have the level of experience and expertise you require. They should belong to an appropriate professional or self-regulatory body.

Services offered vary, and can include advice on how to leave your money when you die, tax planning and general strategic planning, as well as advice on investments. The activities of both groups are controlled and supervised by their professional organizations.

INSURANCE ADVISERS

Insurance advisers come into their own in the area of life assurance and pensions. They now have to decide whether they are company representatives or independent insurance brokers. To be the latter they must meet certain conditions and must register with the Insurance Brokers' Registration Council.

They offer you – in addition to advice on life assurance and pensions – advice on general insurance matters (relating to your home, car, etc.), tax advice, portfolio management services and advice on unit trusts.

STOCKBROKERS

If you want advice about shares, British government stocks, unit trusts or management of your investments (if you have a substantial sum, more than, say, £10,000) you should familiarize yourself with how stockbrokers work.

They are members of the Stock Exchange and are bound by a number of rules. They offer you many services in connection with the choice of investments and the management of them.

INVESTMENT ADVISERS

Investment advisers offer you general advice; they may be useful if you want to invest a lump sum. Their charges vary. In the past it has been difficult to find out how much they are paid and by whom; in future, though, you should be able to find out. If you are asked for a fee, check what it will cover.

Services offered vary. They can include general investment advice, complete management of your portfolio with discretion to buy and sell investments without referring to you, advice on tax and pensions, management of a lump sum investment for you and access to many specialist savings and investment products, such as unit trusts, insurance bonds, offshore funds and the like.

Don't forget, though, that you can go direct to the company. This is worth doing if you know your own mind very well and have become well acquainted with the investment scene. You will be made more than welcome by the company. Don't, however, expect that you will be able to buy more cheaply – the financial world doesn't usually work that way. However, you may be persuasive enough to achieve some financial advantage.

Services on offer from companies include information about the relative merits of their products and the tax implications, and also general information about the financial markets and customer services. You may be invited to attend seminars and be given access to telephone help-lines and the like. Without being too cynical, do remember that they are acting with enlightened self-interest and with the aim that at some point you will buy one or more of their products and services.

OTHER SOURCES OF HELP AND ADVICE

Department of Health and Social Security

Local offices are there to serve you. The staff will help with information and advice, and they have a wide range of useful leaflets on various subjects to help you to sort out your particular problem.

Inland Revenue

Your local tax office has useful information to help you understand your tax position.

Appendix 4

Key organizations

You can get help and advice from many other organizations in the financial services industry and, in particular, through the new self-regulatory structure. Here are some brief details about what the organizations are, what they do and where to contact them.

THE SECURITIES AND INVESTMENTS BOARD (SIB)

This was set up under the Financial Services Act 1986 and is empowered to authorize and regulate investment businesses. Its chairman and members are jointly appointed by the Secretary of State for Trade and Industry and the Governor of the Bank of England. Its composition is supposed to ensure a balance between the interests of investment business and those of the public.

- The Securities and Investments Board, 3 Royal Exchange Buildings, London EC3V 3NL (01–283 2474)

SELF-REGULATORY ORGANIZATIONS (SROs)

These organizations must satisfy the SIB that their rules provide investors with protection equivalent to those of the SIB. Recognized SROs will normally regulate certain types of investment businesses only, and their rules will be required to restrict their members to those types of business, unless they are also members of another SRO. The following are SROs:

- Association of Futures Brokers and Dealers (AFBD), B Section, 5th Floor, Plantation House, 4–16 Mincing Lane, London EC3 3DX (01–626 9763).
  This is the self-regulatory body for investor protection, covering investment management and advice on the commodity and financial futures markets.

- Financial Intermediaries, Managers and Brokers Regulatory Association (FIMBRA), Hertsmere House, Marsh Wall, London E14 9RW (01–538 8860 and 01–895 1229).

    Covers the provision of investment services to retail customers. Most members advise on, and arrange, life and pensions policies and unit trusts. Others offer personal portfolio management services.

- Investment Management Regulatory Organisation (IMRO), Centre Point, 103 New Oxford Street, London WC1A 1PT (01–379 0601).

    Covers investment managers and advisers, including managers and trustees of collective investment schemes and in-house pension managers.

- Life Assurance and Unit Trust Regulatory Organisation (LAUTRO), Centre Point, 103 New Oxford Street, London WC1A 1QH (01–379 0444).

    Covers life companies, friendly societies and unit trust managers engaged in the marketing and selling of insurance-linked investments or units.

- The Securities Association, The Stock Exchange Building, London EC2N 1EQ (01–256 9000).

    Covers firms dealing, broking and advising on international and domestic securities and related options and futures and incidental investment management. Created by a merger of the Stock Exchange and the International Securities Regulatory Organisation.

RECOGNIZED PROFESSIONAL BODIES (RPBs)

The Financial Services Act also makes provision for professional bodies such as the Law Society and the Institute of Chartered Accountants to apply to the SIB for recognition as RPBs.

OTHER IMPORTANT FINANCIAL ORGANIZATIONS

The Association of British Insurers (ABI)

This was established in 1985 and took over the functions

previously performed by several different trade associations. It has two codes of practice, one covering general insurance business and another covering long-term (e.g. life) insurance. Members have to agree to enforce the codes. Unlike the Insurance Ombudsman (see below), the ABI can deal with complaints from third parties about insurance companies.

- The Association of British Insurers, Aldermary House, Queen Street, London EC4 1NTT (01–248 4477).

The Banking Ombudsman scheme

This was established in 1986 to receive unresolved complaints about the provision of banking services to individuals (not companies) and to 'facilitate the satisfaction, settlement or withdrawal of such complaints'. The Ombudsman is appointed by, and is responsible to, the Council of the Office of the Banking Ombudsman. The scheme is paid for by the member banks and is free to its users.

- The Office of the Banking Ombudsman, Citadel House, 5–11 Fetter Lane, London EC4A 1BR.

The Insurance Ombudsman scheme

This was established in 1981 to receive enquiries and complaints about personal insurance policies provided by its member companies. The Ombudsman is responsible to the Insurance Ombudsman Bureau's Council, an independent body representing public and consumer interests. The scheme is paid for by its members and is free to users.

The Ombudsman will deal with your complaint if you are a private policy-holder and your policy was issued in the United Kingdom, the Isle of Man or the Channel Islands. You have to write to, or telephone, the Ombudsman within six months of the date when your insurance company gave you its final decision, giving the company's name and your policy number, and explain the problem. If the Ombudsman can deal with your dispute, he will let you know. In exceptional circumstances the time limit may be waived.

You can either accept the Ombudsman's decision – in which case the company must pay you any award he may have made up to £100,000 (or £10,000 per annum for permanent health insurance matters) and take note of the Ombudsman's recommendations – or you can reject it, in which case the decision is cancelled and you can take legal action. Your legal rights will not have been affected by the Ombudsman's decision or recommendation.

- The Insurance Ombudsman Bureau, 31 Southampton Row, London WC1B 5HT (01–242 8613).

The Unit Trust Ombudsman Scheme

This scheme was established in 1988 to receive enquiries and complaints about unit trusts from personal unit-holders. The Ombudsman is, however, completely independent. The scheme is paid for by the unit trust management companies which are members of the scheme.

- The Unit Trust Ombudsman, 31 Southampton Row, London WC1B 5HJ (01–242 8613).

The British Insurance and Investment Brokers' Association (BIIBA)

This is a trade association representing insurance brokers and investment intermediaries and provides a complaints handling and conciliation service.

- British Insurance and Investment Brokers' Association (BIIBA), BIIBA House, 14 Bevis Marks, London EC3A 7NT (01–623 9043).

The Insurance Brokers Registration Council

This was set up by the Insurance (Registration) Act 1977. The Act provides for the registration of insurance brokers and for the regulation of their professional standards. The Council administers the Act and the rules made under it and publishes a register of individual insurance brokers and a list of enrolled bodies corporate who carry on business as insurance brokers. An insurance broker must meet adequate accounting requirements, have professional indemnity insurance and comply with a code of conduct. Each applicant must demonstrate to the Council that they are entitled to have their name entered in the register under the terms of Section 3 of the Act, not only through experience and qualification but also by demonstrating that they have the character and suitability to be a registered insurance broker.

On 22 January 1988, the Council received authorization by the SIB as a Recognized Professional Body under the Financial Services Act 1986 and now regulates 1,200 firms of insurance brokers in the conduct of their investment business. Further information can be obtained from:

- The Registrar, Insurance Brokers Registration Council, 15 St Helen's Place, London EC3A 6DS.

The Building Societies Ombudsman scheme
This covers the operation of share and deposit accounts, all kinds of loans and credits, money transmission, foreign exchange and agency payments and receipts. The Ombudsman is able to make awards of up to £100,000. Use of the scheme will not prevent you from taking legal action if you disagree with the Ombudsman's decision. The scheme is an outcome of the Building Societies Act 1986. The service is free to users.

- The Building Societies Ombudsman, Grosvenor Gardens House, 35–7 Grosvenor Gardens, London SW1X 7AW (01–931 0011).

The Building Societies Association (BSA)
This is the trade association of building societies.

- The Building Societies Association, 3 Savile Row, London W1X 1AF (01–437 0655).

The Law Society
This is the professional body for solicitors. Its role is to set rules of practice in accordance with the Solicitors Act, to monitor education and training, to act as a lobbying body on behalf of the profession and to set the standards for entry into the profession.

- The Law Society, 113 Chancery Lane, London WC2A 1PL (01–242 1222).

The Institute of Chartered Accountants of England and Wales
This professional body represents 90,000 chartered accountants. It plays a prominent part in equipping its members to meet the

increasing needs of business and of the general public by education and training and the maintenance of the highest standards of
professional conduct and competence. There are similar organizations for Scotland and Northern Ireland.

- Institute of Chartered Accountants of England and Wales
  (ICA), Moorgate Place, London EC2P 2BJ (01–628 7060).

Appendix 5

Financial problems

If you are experiencing financial difficulties and are unsure how to get help, contact your local Citizen's Advice Bureau or Consumer Advice Centre. You may also find a specialist Money Advice Centre in your area (there are about fifteen in the United Kingdom), but generalist advice centres also have specialist money advice workers who can help you with financial problems. Consult the information office of your local authority if you need help in locating advice centres.

Money advice workers are able to help those in debt by, for example, giving assistance in checking tax benefit entitlements, contacting creditors, checking on the planning of expenditure and helping to arrange reasonable repayment programmes. They can also advise on legal procedures.

There are also several financial help-lines you can consult. These include:

1. 01–929 3652 – to check if your investment adviser is authorized. This is the special help-line operated by the SIB.
2. 01–200 3000 – for a list of your ten nearest independent financial advisers. The line is operated by the Campaign for Independent Financial Advice (CAMIFA), which is sponsored by several leading insurance companies.
3. Elsewhere (see Appendix 8) you will find information about other sources of help.

Appendix 6

What every woman needs to know about money

WHAT A WORKING WOMAN COULD EARN

All of us tend to consider our income and expenditure on an annual basis. As well as that, it is worth considering the money which, overall, will pass through a working woman's hands during the course of her working life.

The examples shown here are, necessarily, based on certain assumptions. They have been kept simple, so that they are relevant to most women.

YOUR EARNINGS DURING YOUR WORKING LIFE

Simplified table to find out what you can earn during your working life

| Number of years earning salary | Annual salary | | | | |
	£7,000	£10,000	£15,000	£20,000	£25,000
5	35,000	50,000	75,000	100,000	125,000
10	70,000	100,000	150,000	200,000	250,000
15	105,000	150,000	225,000	300,000	375,000
20	140,000	200,000	300,000	400,000	500,000
25	175,000	250,000	375,000	500,000	625,000
30	210,000	300,000	450,000	600,000	750,000
35	245,000	350,000	525,000	700,000	875,000
40	280,000	400,000	600,000	800,000	1,000,000

In order to use the table, add up the sums appropriate to you.

- If you earned £7,000 per annum when you were 20, rose to £10,000 per annum at 25, and stayed at that level until the age of 60, then you would earn:
  - £7,000 for 5 years   = £35,000
  - £10,000 for 35 years   = £350,000

  - Total over 40 years   = £385,000

- If you were promoted to £20,000 per annum at 30, then to £25,000 per anmum at 35, your earnings would total at 60:
  - £7,000 for 5 years   = £35,000
  - £10,000 for 35 years   = £50,000
  - £20,000 for 5 years   = £100,000
  - £25,000 for 25 years   = £625,000

  - Total over 40 years   = £810,000

If your salary at a particular point falls between two sets of figures shown in the table, make a rough estimate between the two. Make a similar estimate if the length of time for which a particular amount was earned is between two sets of figures.

HOW MONEY GROWS
Most of us probably don't spend enough time in considering how the few £s we save today can grow over a period of, say, five years.

The following examples give simple comparisons between several methods of saving and have been worked out using gross interest, that is, before tax has been deducted. However, remember all banks and building societies normally pay interest net of basic rate tax liability.

- £25 per month saved in a bank deposit account (from 1 July 1983 to 30 June 1988) would have grown to £1,711.40. (The money saved would be £1,500; the interest earned would be £211.40.)
- £1,000 invested in a bank deposit account (from 1 July 1983 to 30 June 1988) would have grown to £1,402.47. (The interest would be £402.47.)

- £2,000 deposited in a high interest cheque account on 14 February 1984 when the account was launched and left in the account until 1 July 1988 would be worth £3,204.99. (The interest would be £1,204.99.)

(Source: Midland Bank)

THE COST OF CREDIT

Most of us succumb all too readily to the temptation of buying now and paying later. The true cost of credit is too often not considered at the time of purchase.

Here are some sobering facts, based on a comparison of bank and credit card interest rates over the last two years.

Comparison of bank and credit card interest rates over the last two years

Bank	Bank personal loan rates (APR)		Credit card rates (APR)	
Barclays	October 1985	22·8	*Barclaycard*	
	April 1986	22·7	March 1985	26·8
	June 1986	19·7	July 1987	23·1
Lloyds	February 1985	23·8	*Lloyds Access*	
	May 1985	23·1	February 1985	26·8
	May 1986	19·5	May 1987	23·8
Midland	January 1985	23·8	*Midland Access*	
	March 1986	21·7	February 1985	26·8
	May 1986	19·7	June 1987	23·1
National Westminster	February 1985	23·0	*NatWest Access*	
	June 1986	20·7	As Midland	
	April 1987	20·7		
	October 1987	20·0		

In the table, we have quoted bank personal loan rates instead of overdraft interest rates. Until very recently overdrafts have not been 'packaged' by the banks and interest rates and fees have been negotiable.

It is noticeable that the banks have slightly different rates at any one time. Therefore, it is not possible to quote a standard figure for bank personal loans.

(Source: Midland Bank)

Store credit cards (correct at 1 August 1988)

	Settled by cheque (APR)	Settled by direct debit (APR)
Dixons	39·8	29·8
Rumbelows	39·2	32·9
Next	32·9	26·8
Marks & Spencers	26·8	26·8

(Source: Midland Bank)

RAINY DAY OR EMERGENCY MONEY

We are all aware of the unexpected emergency, the problem
or opportunity which calls for immediate cash. How much emergency or rainy day money should we keep readily to hand?

The answer to this question, of course, relates to individual
circumstances. As a rule of thumb, the following will act as a
guide:

- *Emergencies*. It is as well to keep £100–£500 where you can get
  at it within a day or so.
- *Larger-scale emergencies*. You may suddenly need to pay, for
  example, for a new roof on the house, an operation, a major
  car repair or an air ticket. These could require two sources of
  finance – cash and credit. It would help, therefore, if you have
  access to £1,000 or more within, say, seven days. It would also
  help if you are not borrowing to the limit on your mortgage,
  credit cards and other facilities. Try to be sure you can always
  borrow £2,500 or more quickly and easily. Gold cards usually
  make an automatic overdraft provision for emergencies such as
  the ones mentioned here.

PENSION PROVISION

How much provision should you aim for to ensure yourself a
reasonably financially trouble-free retirement?

The answer to this question will necessarily differ from person
to person, depending on circumstances. Here are some facts to
take into consideration.

Life after work

To be sure you are safe in your planning, assume you will live to
100! This is some 40 years after the current retirement age for a
woman, a sobering thought. It is considered by medical experts

that more and more women will be receiving their royal congra-
tulatory telegrams on their hundredth birthdays as the years go
by.

Money requirements after work

While it is recognized that expenditure drops with age because
responsibilities for children, holidays and home maintenance costs
are reduced, it is as well to be aware that other costs could
increase. These include health costs, cost of caring services and
the like.

As a general rule, plan for an income of at least 50 per cent of
your retiring salary for the years after work, and try to protect this
income against inflation. If you can also supplement it with
income from savings, investment or working activities that will be
helpful.

Try to carry on earning for as long as possible. It is important
economically and it will help to keep you young as well.

DHSS BENEFIT RATES

If you think you may qualify for benefits, enquire at your local
DHSS office. The brief information included here will give you
some background. Rates quoted apply from the week beginning
11 April 1988 and last until April 1989. Amounts paid may be
more or less than standard rates, depending on circumstances,
which include individual national insurance contributions.

All the rates shown are weekly unless otherwise stated. The
relevant leaflets to consult for more information are shown.

- *Leaflet CH1, Child Benefit*
  - For each child: £7.25

- *Leaflet NI261, Family Credit*

  - You may be able to get some Family Credit if your income
    (explained in leaflet FC1) after tax and national insurance is
    less than £96.50. This limit is increased by the following
    allowances for children:

Under 11:	£8.50
11–15:	£16.00
16–17:	£21.00
18:	£30.50

    To make this clear, if you have a child under 11, you may be

able to get some Family Credit if your income (after tax and national insurance) is less than £105.00.

- You may be able to get the maximum amount of Family Credit if your net income is less than £51.45 per week. The maximum rate is as follows:

Adult credit (amount per parent):	£32.10
For each child aged under 11:	£6.05
For each child aged 11–15:	£11.40
For each child aged 16–17:	£14.70
For each child aged 18:	£21.35

- *Leaflet NI14, Guardian's Allowance*
  - For each child: £8.40

- *Leaflet RR1, Housing Benefit*
  - The maximum Housing Benefit you can get is 100 per cent of your eligible rent and 80 per cent of your eligible rates.
    Deductions for non-dependants

Taken from rent rebates and allowances for those aged 18 or over and in remunerative work:	£8.20
Boarders:	£8.20
Others:	£3.45
Low earnings threshold:	£49.20
Taken from rates rebates for those aged 18 or over:	£3.00

    Premium

Lone parent (Housing Benefit):	£8.60

    Amenity deductions

Heating:	£6.70
Hot water:	£0.80
Lighting:	£0.50
Cooking:	£0.80
All fuels:	£8.80

- *Leaflet NI17A, Maternity Allowance*
  - Maternity Allowance: £31.30

- *Leaflet CH11, One-Parent Benefit*
  - One-Parent Benefit: £4.90

- *Leaflet SB16, Social Fund*
  - This provides lump sum payments. Savings of £500 or more are taken into account. Most grants and loans from the Social Fund are discretionary.

Maternity Payment: £85.00
Funeral Payment: Up to the cost of a simple funeral

- *Leaflet NI17A, Statutory Maternity Pay*
  - If your average weekly earnings are £41 a week or over:
    Higher rate: 90 per cent of your average earnings
    Lower rate: £34.25

- *Leaflet NP45, Widow's Benefit*
  - Widow's Payment (lump sum):   £1,000
    Widowed Mother's Allowance   £41.15
    Widow's Pension (standard rate):   £41.15
    Age-related Widow's Benefit
    The payment depends on your age at the time of your
    husband's death or when the Widowed Mother's Allowance
    stops. See the ages below; refer to the ages in brackets if you
    became entitled before 11 April 1988.

54(49):	£38.27	49(44):	£23.87
53(48):	£35.39	48(43):	£20.99
52(47):	£32.51	47(42):	£18.11
51(46):	£29.63	46(41):	£15.23
50(45):	£26.75	45(40):	£12.35

- *Leaflet NI16A, Invalidity Benefit*
  - *Invalidity allowance*
    Higher rate: £8.65
    Middle rate: £5.50
    Lower rate: £2.75
    Basic invalidity pension: £41.15
    Additional invalidity pension
    Your additional invalidity pension depends on your con-
    tributions to the state earnings related pension scheme
    (SERPS) since April 1978.

- *Leaflet NI212, Invalid Care Allowance (ICA)*
  - ICA: £24.75

Appendix 7

Glossary

Often you come across words which you don't understand when you are handling money matters. Those dealing with you seem to take it for granted that you understand, but you don't. In this glossary some key terms are explained to help you make some sense of the jargon.

Annual percentage rate (APR)
A way of expressing the true cost of borrowing which enables consumers to make comparisons between lenders.

Annuity
A form of life assurance that, like a pension, provides for a sum of money to be paid to you at regular intervals if you are a policy-holder.

Arrears
The amount of money which has become due for payment under an agreement and has not been paid.

Assets
What you own. These may include the money value of your house, car, furniture etc. (called 'fixed assets'); money and its equivalent, such as your investments and savings (called 'liquid assets' because you can turn them into money and spend them) and special skills or the goodwill of, for example, a shop which you own (called 'intangible assets' because you can use them to earn money).

Assurance
An arrangement by which something is promised or guaranteed. The word most commonly appears in the term 'life assurance', which means that money will be paid on death.

Authorized unit trust
A unit trust scheme authorized by the Department of Trade. Only authorized unit trusts can be offered for sale to the general public.

Balance
The total amount remaining to be paid under an agreement.

Bank Giro
A system which allows money transfers between the British clearing banks.

Bears
Pessimistic investors on the Stock Exchange who believe that share prices will fall.

Benefit
The money paid by an insurance company when a claim is made.

Bid price
The price which a unit trust management company will pay for the units you sell back to it.

Blue chips
These are securities and shares with the highest status as investments, particularly in the industrial markets.

Bonus
The extra amount of money paid with the final benefit to a policy-holder who has a with-profits policy.

Broker
An agent who, in return for a fee or commission, buys or sells goods, securities, insurance, etc. for you.

Budget
A financial plan of a government, company or individual for a period ahead, say a month or a year. A budget includes forecasts of spending and income. It is (or should be) flexible so that it can be adjusted as time goes on, as actual figures come in or circumstances alter forecasts up or down. The national Budget is

presented in parliament every March by the Chancellor of the Exchequer. Your own budget is just as important to you.

Bulls
Investors or speculators on the Stock Exchange who invest in the expectation that share prices will rise.

Completion
When purchasing or selling a property, the final date on which the necessary documents are transferred from one owner to another in return for the price paid for the property.

Covenants
A legally binding agreement to do something, usually to make a series of payments to another person or organization. Charities may recover income tax on payments made under covenants lasting for four or more years, and the higher rate taxpayer may also claim back some tax on covenanted payments. Tax is no longer recoverable on covenanted payments between individuals, but the recipient can still claim tax deducted by the payer on those which started before 15 March 1988.

Creditor
A person to whom money is owed.

Debtor
A person who owes money to you.

Deflation
Falling prices and incomes.

Endowment assurance
Type of life assurance policy which provides a sum of money either at the end of an agreed period of time or on the death of the policy-holder, whichever happens first.

Equities
The ordinary shares of a limited company which entitle holders to a share of the profits and the company assets after all liabilities have been met.

Equity
The goodwill and assets of a company after all liabilities have been deducted. Also the interest of an ordinary shareholder in a company (see 'Equities'); and a home-owner's share of the value of their home: that is, the value of the home less the outstanding mortgage.

ERNIE
Electronic Random Number Indicator Equipment, the computer that picks Premium Bond winners.

Exchange of contracts
The point when a property transaction become legally binding on both buyer and seller (in England and Wales). Up to this point, either party may withdraw from the deal.

Executor
The person appointed to administer a dead person's will.

Face value
The apparent value, printed or written on a document such as a £1 note or a bond. The market value is not always the face value.

Financial or fiscal year
An accounting year. In Britain, the government's financial year is from 1 April to 31 March of the following year but the fiscal year is generally from 6 April to 5 April of the following year.

Fiscal policy
The government's financial policy, especially the way it raises tax revenue and influences the level of business and financial activity of us all.

Fringe benefits
Payments 'in kind' or what an employee gets on top of regular earnings from an employer, such as a company car, medical insurance or meal vouchers. These must be declared on your tax return.

***FT*-SE Index, *FT*-SE 100-Share Index**
The most commonly used indices for measuring movements in the

Stock Market – the *FT*-SE Index is based on thirty key companies' shares and the *FT*-SE 100-Share Index on a hundred key companies' shares. (*FT* stands for *The Financial Times*.)

Gilt
Abbreviation for 'gilt-edged', the highest quality securities in the UK. The term normally applies only to government stocks, which are gilt-edged as there is virtually no default risk attached to them.

Indemnity
A guaranteed compensation for loss. It can also mean the legal exemption from liabilities resulting from actions or defaults.

Insurance
A service that offers a policy-holder financial protection against specified events (such as death while travelling, or loss or damage to property) that may occur.

Insurance broker
An insurance broker advises on and arranges policies which are offered by many different companies.

Interest
Amount charged for the use of credit or borrowed money. Also known as a service charge or hire purchase charge.

Interest rate
A percentage charged for borrowing money, usually so much per cent per year or per month. Interest rates add up quickly: interest rates on a bank overdraft or credit card loan may not seem much, but the interest you pay builds up rapidly even over short periods.

Investment
Money of yours that is now used by others to provide interest income for benefits and advantages for you in the future.

Liquidity
Cash, or assets which you can turn into cash. Cash is 'liquid'.

Market value
The amount that can be got on the open, competitive market for the sale of a property, asset, goods, service, etc.

Maturity date
An agreed date in the future when an insurance policy comes to an end. No further payments are made after that date and the benefit is paid by the assurance company.

Mortgage
A way of buying a house through a building society, bank or other lender, who is known as the mortgagee. The house 'belongs' to the mortgagee as a security for the money they have lent you (the mortgagor) until you have paid everything off (including the interest). Then the house becomes yours.

Nominal charge
A fee that is minimal in comparison with the real worth of something, usually a service.

Offshore fund
A fund established outside the UK (in this case excluding the Channel Islands and the Isle of Man). These funds are run on broad unit trust principles but are not authorized or controlled by the Department of Trade. They vary in their adherence to the standards of UK unit trust practice.

Overdraft
The amount of money you owe your bank when you have taken more money out of your account than you had in it. You will have to pay interest on your overdraft and you should always ask your bank manager before overdrawing. They will usually let you overdraw if they believe you will be able to repay the money in due course.

PAYE (Pay As You Earn)
The system by which income is deducted from wages and salaries by employers and paid to the government.

Portfolio
An investment term for all the securities belonging to any one owner.

Premium
The amount you pay above the normal price level. This may reflect the current market conditions. In insurance, the premium is the amount you pay, usually in irregular instalments, for an insurance policy.

Proposal form
The form completed by a person who is seeking assurance or insurance.

Pushing shares
Talking enthusiastically about a share so that its price rises.

Rat race
The blind pursuit of success.

Rebate
An allowance or refund against the cost of a service, subject to agreement.

Redundancy
The term used to mean that the job itself is disappearing and therefore there is no need for the employee's services in future.

Revolving credit
A system of credit whereby further borrowing up to an agreed limit is permitted at any time.

Security
A guarantee of the subsequent return of a specified amount of cash. Remember that a security does not necessarily provide you with the same amount of security as the purchasing power of the money invested. It also does not necessarily give you protection against inflation.

Speculation
Gambling or buying in the hope of making financial gain.

Stag
An investor who wants to make a 'quick buck' and buys new issue shares, hoping to sell them quickly for profit.

Tax avoidance
Legal avoidance of taxes. For instance, you can legally avoid paying tax on articles you buy entirely for business use, providing you satisfy the rules laid down by the Inland Revenue.

Tax evasion
The illegal avoidance of paying tax which you are required by law to pay.

True rate of interest
The rate of interest which takes account of the reducing amount of capital outstanding, usually on a mortgage.

Unit-linked plan
A life assurance policy under which the premiums paid are invested in a unit-linked insurance fund or a unit trust. Its value fluctuates with the price of units.

Unit trust
A fund of investment in stocks and shares managed by professional investment managers. The investments of the trust are held by an independent trustee, usually a major bank or insurance company. Each unit represents an equal share in the assets of the trust and can be purchased or sold directly through the managers or indirectly through a professional intermediary. The value of each unit reflects movements in the value of the trust's investments and is not influenced by purchase and sales of units.

Utmost good faith (uberrimae fides)
When this phrase is used it is understood that a proposer or a policy-holder is always completely honest and truthful in dealings with an insurance or assurance company. It is one of the principles or rules to be observed by both sides in the contract.

Whole life assurance
The type of policy that provides for an agreed sum of money to be paid to the policy-holder's family or next-of-kin when the policy-holder dies.

With-profits policy

This is a special arrangement that can be made with an assurance or insurance company for an endowment policy or a whole-life policy. If a with-profits arrangement is made, the policy-holder shares in the profits that the company makes. These are added to the benefit which is finally paid out. The arrangement must be made at the time of taking out the policy and, naturally, the premiums are a little higher.

Yield

The phrase used to express the annual return from an investment.

Appendix 8

Further information

SPECIAL ORGANIZATIONS FOR WOMEN – AND OTHERS

Women have always been very good at organizing things for themselves. Today there are in the UK many women's organizations, some of which have great influence in national and even international affairs. They are all particularly good at relating to the needs and priorities of an individual and, in addition, most are friendly and welcoming. There are also many similar organizations for both women and men. Here is a list of some of the key organizations effective in business, financial and community affairs.

- Age Concern, 60 Pitcairn Road, Mitcham, Surrey CR4 3LL.
  Aims to improve the lives of elderly people by providing direct services through own local network and old people's welfare organizations. Publications and handbooks are available for the elderly and those caring for them; queries relating to elderly people answered.
- Association of Inner Wheel Clubs, 51 Warwick Street, London SW1V 2AT.
- The Association of Women Solicitors, 8 Breams Buildings, London EC4A 1HP.
- British Federation of University Women, Cheyne Walk, London SW3 5BA.
- British Institute of Management (BIM), Management House, Cottingham Road, Corby, Northamptonshire NN17 1TT.
- City Women's Network, 20 Essex Street, London WC2R 3AL.
- Consumer's Association, 2 Marylebone Road, London NW1 4DX.
  Main activities are campaigning for improvements in goods and services, undertaking research and carrying out comparative testing of goods and services. Publisher of *Which?* and other guides.

- Equal Opportunities Commission, 1 Bedford Street, London WC2RE 9HD. Will supply lists of courses intended for women.
- Independent Schools Information Service, 56 Buckingham Gate, London SE1E 6AG.
- Institute of Trading Standards Administration (ITSA), Department of Trading Standards, County Offices, Kendal, Cumbria LA9 4RQ.
  Professional body for trading standards officers, responsible for standards of conduct and discipline, enforcing the law with regard to standards of quality, quantity and some aspects of safety and price; advises public on problems encountered in everyday commercial transactions.
- International Federation of Business and Professional Women, Buchanan House, 24–30 Holborn, London EC1N 2HS.
- Manpower Services Commission, Head Office, Moorfoot, Sheffield S1 4PQ.
  Provides lists of contact groups and courses for women trainees.
- National Association of Ladies Circles, Provincial House, Cooke Street, Keighley, West Yorkshire BD21 3NN.
- National Association of Women's Clubs, 5 Vernon Rise, Kings Cross Road, London WC1X 9EP.
- National Consumer Council, 20 Grosvenor Gardens, London SW1W 0DH.
  Aims 'to promote the interests of consumers to ensure that those who make decisions which affect consumers take a balanced view. Works on variety of projects including nutrition labelling, debt, financial services and data protection.
- National Federation of Women's Institutes, 39 Eccleston Street, London SW1 9NT.
- National Union of Townswomen's Guilds, Chamber of Commerce House, 75 Harbourne Road, Birmingham B15 3DA.
- Network, 25 Park Road, London NW1 6XN.
  The association for women in the professions, commerce, industry and the arts.
- Office of Fair Trading (OFT), Field House, Breams Building, London EC4A 1RP.
  Consumer Affairs Division of OFT monitors trade practices affecting the consumer, encouraging trade and industry to adopt a code of trading practice which is fair to firms and consumers. Publishes wide range of booklets on its work.

- The Pepperell Unit, The Industrial Society, Robert Hyde House, 48 Bryanston Square, London W1H 7LN.
  Runs a variety of courses and workshops for women, aimed at enhancing women's talents and self-development.
- Small Business Bureau, 32 Smith Square, London SW1P 3HH. National Co-ordinator: Irene Jeffrey.
- Soroptomists International, 63 Bayswater Road, London W2 3PJ.
  An organization for women of achievement.
- The 300 Group, 9 Poland Street, London W1V 3DG.
  A non-party group formed in 1980 to seek the equal representation of women in parliament, and to encourage and train women to seek and hold public and political office. Many active regional groups.
- United Kingdom Federation of Business and Professional Women, 23 Ansdell Street, London W8 5BN.
- United Kingdom Home Economics Federation, 9 Alms Hill Crescent, Sheffield S11 9QZ.
- Women in Enterprise, 26 Bond Street, Wakefield WF1 2QP.
  Aims to provide information for aspiring female entrepreneurs or small businesswomen on finance and sources of advice, to develop and promote training programmes, and also to persuade educational establishments, business schools and enterprise agencies to look at running a business from a woman's point of view as well as a man's. Baroness Seear is chief patron.
- Women in Management (WIM), 64 Marryatt Road, London SW19 5BN.
  Publishes three newsletters a year; periodically holds major events, regular discussion evenings and executive lunches for senior women.

FURTHER READING, ETC.

Margaret Allen, *The Hutchinson Money Minder* (Hutchinson).

Rosemary Burr, *Make Your Money Work* (Rosters Ltd).

Rosemary Burr, *Sticky Fingers* (Rosters Ltd). How to be ripped-off – and enjoy it!

Robert B. Davies, *A Layman's Guide to Profitable Letting* (Jofleur Publications).

Margaret Dibben, *Guardian Money Guide* (Guardian Newspapers).

Helen Franks (ed.), *What Every Woman Should Know About Retirement* (Age Concern).

Derrick Hanson, *Money Guide* (Kluwer). This provides a useful update service.

Jennifer Hurstfield, *Part-Timers Under Pressure* (Low Pay Unit).

David Lewis, *The Savers And Investors Guide 1988/89* (Wisebuy Publications).

Anthea Masey, *How To Become A Woman Of Substance* (Judy Piatkus (Publishers) Ltd).

Martin Rathfelder, *How To Claim State Benefits* (Northcote House).

Edith Rudinger, *The Which? Book of Insurance* (Consumers' Association).

Sue Thomas, *Family Finance* (Woodhead-Faulkner).

Henry Toch, *How To Pay Less Income Tax* (Pitman Publishing Ltd).

Sara Williams, *Small Business Guide* (Penguin Books).

Diana Wright, *A Consumer Guide To Buying And Selling A Home* (Daily Telegraph).

Equal Pay For Equal Value. Equal Opportunities Commission. A guide to the amended Equal Pay Act; free booklet.

Equality At Work. Equal Opportunities Commission. A guide to the employment provisions of the Sex Discrimination Act 1975; free booklet.

Fair Dealing. Equal Opportunities Commission. Guidance on the Sex Discrimination Act for employment services.

Family Law – Transfer of Money Between Spouses – The Married Woman's Property Act 1964. Law Commission Working Paper No. 90.

The Money Mail Insurance Guide (The Daily Mail).

Pensions For Women. Company Pensions Information Centre. Free of charge.

Which? Way To Buy, Sell And Move House. Consumers' Association.

Women & Pensions. Age Concern and Equal Opportunities Commission. Obtainable from the Equal Opportunities Commission; free of charge.

The Children's Society produces three leaflets about divorce and separation. *Divorce And You* (60p) is designed to help children and young people sort out their feelings about divorce. *Divorce And Your Children* (20p) is for parents; it offers simple guidelines to what children need and lists organizations and publications which can help. *Divorce And The Family* (50p) is aimed at those whose work brings them into contact with families experiencing divorce and separation but who may not have had formal training in counselling.

A complete range of literature about tax legislation is available from all Inland Revenue offices. Publications cover all aspects of tax legislation, including married women and self-employment.

Magazines (all monthly)
What Investment
Choice (for retirement planning)
Money Observer
Your Money & Family Wealth

Newspapers
A growing number of daily and Sunday newspapers feature regular personal and family money pages. These include:
- Wednesdays. *Daily Mail, Daily Express, Today, Daily Mirror.*
- Saturdays. *Times, Daily Telegraph, Guardian, Independent, Financial Times.*
- Sundays. *Sunday Times, Observer, Sunday Telegraph, Mail On Sunday, Sunday Express.*

Broadcast programmes
Money Box (Radio 4)
Moneyspinner (Channel 4)
Money Programme (BBC 2)

Booklets and leaflets
These following organizations produce several publications about the types of savings and investments shown.

National savings
Department for National Savings, Freepost 4335, Bristol BS1 3YX (or from post offices)

Insurance-linked schemes
Association of British Insurers, Aldermary House, Queen Street, London EC4 1NTT

Banks
Banking Information Service, 10 Lombard Street, London EC3V
9AT

Building societies
Building Societies Association, 3 Savile Row, London W1X 1AF

Unit trusts
Unit Trust Association Information Unit, 65 Kingsway, London
WC28 6TD

Stocks and shares
The Stock Exchange, Public Affairs Department, Old Broad
Street, London EC2N 1HP

Investment trusts
Association of Investment Trust Companies, 6th Floor, Park
House, 16 Finsbury Circus, London EC2M 7JJ

Accountants
Institute of Chartered Accountants of England and Wales, Char-
tered Acountants Hall, PO Box 433, Moorgate Place, London
EC2P 2BJ

All these organizations are corporate associate members of the
Money Management Council.

FOR THE BEST IN PAPERBACKS, LOOK FOR THE

In every corner of the world, on every subject under the sun, Penguin represents quality and variety – the very best in publishing today.

For complete information about books available from Penguin – including Pelicans, Puffins, Peregrines and Penguin Classics – and how to order them, write to us at the appropriate address below. Please note that for copyright reasons the selection of books varies from country to country.

In the United Kingdom: For a complete list of books available from Penguin in the U.K., please write to *Dept E.P., Penguin Books Ltd, Harmondsworth, Middlesex, UB7 0DA*

In the United States: For a complete list of books available from Penguin in the U.S., please write to *Dept BA, Penguin, 299 Murray Hill Parkway, East Rutherford, New Jersey 07073*

In Canada: For a complete list of books available from Penguin in Canada, please write to *Penguin Books Canada Ltd, 2801 John Street, Markham, Ontario L3R 1B4*

In Australia: For a complete list of books available from Penguin in Australia, please write to the *Marketing Department, Penguin Books Australia Ltd, P.O. Box 257, Ringwood, Victoria 3134*

In New Zealand: For a complete list of books available from Penguin in New Zealand, please write to the *Marketing Department, Penguin Books (NZ) Ltd, Private Bag, Takapuna, Auckland 9*

In India: For a complete list of books available from Penguin, please write to *Penguin Overseas Ltd, 706 Eros Apartments, 56 Nehru Place, New Delhi, 110019*

In Holland: For a complete list of books available from Penguin in Holland, please write to *Penguin Books Nederland B.V., Postbus 195, NL–1380AD Weesp, Netherlands*

In Germany: For a complete list of books available from Penguin, please write to *Penguin Books Ltd, Friedrichstrasse 10 – 12, D–6000 Frankfurt Main 1, Federal Republic of Germany*

In Spain: For a complete list of books available from Penguin in Spain, please write to *Longman Penguin España, Calle San Nicolas 15, E–28013 Madrid, Spain*

A CHOICE OF PENGUINS

An African Winter Preston King With an Introduction by Richard Leakey

This powerful and impassioned book offers a unique assessment of the interlocking factors which result in the famines of Africa and argues that there *are* solutions and we *can* learn from the mistakes of the past.

Jean Rhys: Letters 1931–66
Edited by Francis Wyndham and Diana Melly

'Eloquent and invaluable . . . her life emerges, and with it a portrait of an unexpectedly indomitable figure' – Marina Warner in the *Sunday Times*

Among the Russians Colin Thubron

One man's solitary journey by car across Russia provides an enthralling and revealing account of the habits and idiosyncrasies of a fascinating people. 'He sees things with the freshness of an innocent and the erudition of a scholar' – *Daily Telegraph*

The Amateur Naturalist Gerald Durrell with Lee Durrell

'Delight . . . on every page . . . packed with authoritative writing, learning without pomposity . . . it represents a real bargain' – *The Times Educational Supplement*. 'What treats are in store for the average British household' – *Books and Bookmen*

The Democratic Economy Geoff Hodgson

Today, the political arena is divided as seldom before. In this exciting and original study, Geoff Hodgson carefully examines the claims of the rival doctrines and exposes some crucial flaws.

They Went to Portugal Rose Macaulay

An exotic and entertaining account of travellers to Portugal from the pirate-crusaders, through poets, aesthetes and ambassadors, to the new wave of romantic travellers. A wonderful mixture of literature, history and adventure, by one of our most stylish and seductive writers.

FOR THE BEST IN PAPERBACKS, LOOK FOR THE 🐧

A CHOICE OF PENGUINS AND PELICANS

A Question of Economics   Peter Donaldson

Twenty key issues – the City, trade unions, 'free market forces' and many others – are presented clearly and fully in this major book based on a television series.

The Economist Economics   Rupert Pennant-Rea and Clive Crook

Based on a series of 'briefs' published in the *Economist* in 1984, this important new book makes the key issues of contemporary economic thinking accessible to the general reader.

The Tyranny of the Status Quo   Milton and Rose Friedman

Despite the rhetoric, big government has actually *grown* under Reagan and Thatcher. The Friedmans consider why this is – and what we can do now to change it.

Business Wargames   Barrie G. James

Successful companies use military strategy to win. Barrie James shows how – and draws some vital lessons for today's manager.

Atlas of Management Thinking   Edward de Bono

This fascinating book provides a vital repertoire of non-verbal images – to help activate the right side of any manager's brain.

The Winning Streak   Walter Goldsmith and David Clutterbuck

A brilliant analysis of what Britain's best-run and successful companies have in common – a must for all managers.

A CHOICE OF PENGUINS AND PELICANS

Lateral Thinking for Management   Edward de Bono

Creativity and lateral thinking can work together for managers in developing new products or ideas; Edward de Bono shows how.

Understanding Organizations   Charles B. Handy

Of practical as well as theoretical interest, this book shows how general concepts can help solve specific organizational problems.

The Art of Japanese Management   Richard Tanner Pascale and Anthony G. Athos   With an Introduction by Sir Peter Parker

Japanese industrial success owes much to Japanese management techniques, which we in the West neglect at our peril. The lessons are set out in this important book.

My Years with General Motors   Alfred P. Sloan   With an Introduction by John Egan

A business classic by the man who took General Motors to the top – and kept them there for decades.

Introducing Management   Ken Elliott and Peter Lawrence (eds.)

An important and comprehensive collection of texts on modern management which draw some provocative conclusions.

English Culture and the Decline of the Industrial Spirit   Martin J. Wiener

A major analysis of why the 'world's first industrial nation has never been comfortable with industrialism'. 'Very persuasive' – Anthony Sampson in the *Observer*

FOR THE BEST IN PAPERBACKS, LOOK FOR THE

PENGUIN REFERENCE BOOKS

The Penguin English Dictionary

Over 1,000 pages long and with over 68,000 definitions, this cheap, compact and totally up-to-date book is ideal for today's needs. It includes many technical and colloquial terms, guides to pronunciation and common abbreviations.

The Penguin Reference Dictionary

The ideal comprehensive guide to written and spoken English the world over, with detailed etymologies and a wide selection of colloquial and idiomatic usage. There are over 100,000 entries and thousands of examples of how words are actually used – all clear, precise and up-to-date.

The Penguin English Thesaurus

This unique volume will increase anyone's command of the English language and build up your word power. Fully cross-referenced, it includes synonyms of every kind (formal or colloquial, idiomatic and figurative) for almost 900 headings. It is a must for writers and utterly fascinating for any English speaker.

The Penguin Dictionary of Quotations

A treasure-trove of over 12,000 new gems and old favourites, from Aesop and Matthew Arnold to Xenophon and Zola.

The Penguin Wordmaster Dictionary   Manser and Turton

This dictionary puts the pleasure back into word-seeking. Every time you look at a page you get a bonus – a panel telling you everything about a particular word or expression. It is, therefore, a dictionary to be read as well as used for its concise and up-to-date definitions.

FOR THE BEST IN PAPERBACKS, LOOK FOR THE

PENGUIN REFERENCE BOOKS

The Penguin Guide to the Law

This acclaimed reference book is designed for everyday use, and forms the most comprehensive handbook ever published on the law as it affects the individual.

The Penguin Medical Encyclopedia

Covers the body and mind in sickness and in health, including drugs, surgery, history, institutions, medical vocabulary and many other aspects. 'Highly commendable' – *Journal of the Institute of Health Education*

The Penguin French Dictionary

This invaluable French-English, English-French dictionary includes both the literary and dated vocabulary needed by students, and the up-to-date slang and specialized vocabulary (scientific, legal, sporting, etc) needed in everyday life. As a passport to the French language, it is second to none.

A Dictionary of Literary Terms

Defines over 2,000 literary terms (including lesser known, foreign language and technical terms) explained with illustrations from literature past and present.

The Penguin Map of Europe

Covers all land eastwards to the Urals, southwards to North Africa and up to Syria, Iraq and Iran. Scale – 1:5,500,000, 4-colour artwork. Features main roads, railways, oil and gas pipelines, plus extra information including national flags, currencies and populations.

The Penguin Dictionary of Troublesome Words

A witty, straightforward guide to the pitfalls and hotly disputed issues in standard written English, illustrated with examples and including a glossary of grammatical terms and an appendix on punctuation.

FOR THE BEST IN PAPERBACKS, LOOK FOR THE 🐧

PENGUIN DICTIONARIES

Archaeology

Architecture

Art and Artists

Biology

Botany

Building

Chemistry

Civil Engineering

Commerce

Computers

Decorative Arts

Design and Designers

Economics

English and European
  History

English Idioms

Geography

Geology

Historical Slang

Literary Terms

Mathematics

Microprocessors

Modern History 1789–1945

Modern Quotations

Physical Geography

Physics

Political Quotations

Politics

Proverbs

Psychology

Quotations

Religions

Saints

Science

Sociology

Surnames

Telecommunications

The Theatre

Troublesome Words

Twentieth Century History

FOR THE BEST IN PAPERBACKS, LOOK FOR THE 🐧

PENGUIN BUSINESS

Great management classics of the world (with brand new Introductions by leading contemporary figures); widely studied business textbooks; and exciting new business titles covering all the major areas of interest for today's businessman and businesswoman.

Parkinson's Law or **The Pursuit of Progress**   C. Northcote Parkinson
My Years with General Motors   Alfred P. Sloan Jr
Self-Help   Samuel Smiles
The Spirit of Enterprise   George Gilder
Dinosaur & Co: Studies in Corporate Evolution   Tom Lloyd
Understanding Organizations   Charles B. Handy
The Art of Japanese Management   Richard Tanner Pascale & Anthony G. Athos
Modern Management Methods   Ernest Dale & L. C. Michelon
Lateral Thinking for Management   Edward de Bono
The Winning Streak Workout Book   Walter Goldsmith & David Clutterbuck
The Social Psychology of Industry   J. A. C. Brown
Offensive Marketing   J. H. Davidson
The Anatomy of Decisions   Peter G. Moore & H. Thomas
The Human Side of Enterprise   Douglas McGregor
Corporate Recovery   Stuart Slatter